Current
CONTROVERSIES

Mobile Apps

Other Books in the Current Controversies Series

Mobile Apps

Sylvia Engdahl, Book Editor

GREENHAVEN PRESS

A part of Gale, Cengage Learning

GALE
CENGAGE Learning·

Detroit • New York • San Francisco • New Haven, Conn • Waterville, Maine • London

Elizabeth Des Chenes, *Director, Content Strategy*
Cynthia Sanner, *Publisher*
Douglas Dentino, *Manager, New Product*

For more information, contact:
Greenhaven Press
27500 Drake Rd.
Farmington Hills, MI 48331-3535
Or you can visit our Internet site at gale.cengage.com

For product information and technology assistance, contact us at

Gale Customer Support, 1-800-877-4253
For permission to use material from this text or product, submit all requests online at
www.cengage.com/permissions

Further permissions questions can be emailed to permissionrequest@cengage.com

Articles in Greenhaven Press anthologies are often edited for length to meet page requirements. In addition, original titles of these works are changed to clearly present the main thesis and to explicitly indicate the author's opinion. Every effort is made to ensure that Greenhaven Press accurately reflects the original intent of the authors. Every effort has been made to trace the owners of copyrighted material.

Cover image copyright © Umberto Shtanzman/Shutterstock.com.

LIBRARY OF CONGRESS CATALOGING-IN-PUBLICATION DATA

Mobile apps / Sylvia Engdahl, book editor.
    pages cm. -- (Current controversies)
    Includes bibliographical references and index.
    ISBN 978-0-7377-6890-9 (hardcover) -- ISBN 978-0-7377-6891-6 (paperback)
    1. Mobile computing. 2. Application software. 3. Mobile computing--Social aspects. 4. Application software--Social aspects. I. Engdahl, Sylvia.
    QA76.59.M625 2014
    005.3--dc23
                             2013029964

Printed in the United States of America
1 2 3 4 5   18 17 16 15 14

Contents

There is no need for legislation to ban the misuse of geolocation data by apps, as most developers are using it responsibly and the software industry is working to develop privacy guidelines in order to maintain consumer confidence. Location information enables apps to provide innovative features that users value, as shown by their increasing use of them.

Chapter 2: Should Controversial Mobile Apps Be Taken Off the Market?

**Yes: Apps with Offensive Content Should Be
Removed from App Stores**

Theodore Kruczek

Whether or not a person approves of censorship, a store's
policy of not selling apps that contain content it finds
objectionable should be supported because a company
has a right to operate in a way that meets its own goals.
Competition encourages new development; people who
want the option of a censored store should have it, and
those who dislike the policy should buy elsewhere.

Truth Wins Out

More than one hundred-fifty thousand people signed a
petition demanding removal of an app that claimed homosexuality could be "cured." The app, which was aimed
at recruiting clients for "therapy" that medical associations consider damaging, offended many and was in violation of the app store's own policy of rejecting defamatory or offensive apps or those likely to cause harm.

**No: Free Speech Is More Important Than
Eliminating Offensive App Content**

Mitch Wagner

There have been complaints of campaign apps being rejected on a politically-biased basis on grounds that they
contain "defamatory" statements about opponents, although such statements are common in political speeches.
Some have also been rejected because of religious bias. It
is legal for stores to do this but they ought not to, even if
they do block those with adult content.

John Paul Titlow

An app critical of US drone strikes in Pakistan has been rejected although it contains no information that is not already available in news apps; despite the fact that use of apps by foreign dissidents critical of their governments is encouraged. Stores should not reject apps because of their content unless they are obscene, libelous, or in violation of copyright law.

A major app store is selective with regard to what apps are sold in its store, attempting to ensure freedom from porn. However, it has applied this policy inconsistently. It has rejected some apps while accepting others that are equally explicit, and has rescinded some rejections after public outcry. It will lose business if it fails to stay in touch with what its customers want.

Chapter 3: Why Are Web-Based Mobile Apps Overtaking Native Mobile Apps?

With the new technology of the HTML5 programming language, developers can write a web-based mobile app that will run on many devices instead of having to rewrite it as a native app for each device, and it can be easily updated. This is much faster and less expensive, so although native apps make better use of a device's hardware and usually perform better, in the future web apps will prevail.

Native apps run on mobile devices, while cloud apps, a form of web app, run on servers with their data stored in the cloud (that is, on the server), and are accessed by a browser window on the device. Hybrid apps look like native apps to the user, but they are written largely in code that can be used on many devices and are thus less costly to produce and have a longer lifespan.

Chapter 4: What Effect Is the App Economy Having on Society?

Because mobile apps are small and quick to write, individuals, even college students without any money to invest, can produce commercially successful ones. For this reason, the app revolution is developing much faster than the computer revolution of the 1980s did. Small companies are quickly growing into large ones, and many job opportunities are opening up.

Foreword

By definition, controversies are "discussions of questions in which opposing opinions clash" (*Webster's Twentieth Century Dictionary Unabridged*). Few would deny that controversies are a pervasive part of the human condition and exist on virtually every level of human enterprise. Controversies transpire between individuals and among groups, within nations and between nations. Controversies supply the grist necessary for progress by providing challenges and challengers to the status quo. They also create atmospheres where strife and warfare can flourish. A world without controversies would be a peaceful world; but it also would be, by and large, static and prosaic.

The Series' Purpose

The purpose of the Current Controversies series is to explore many of the social, political, and economic controversies dominating the national and international scenes today. Titles selected for inclusion in the series are highly focused and specific. For example, from the larger category of criminal justice, Current Controversies deals with specific topics such as police brutality, gun control, white collar crime, and others. The debates in Current Controversies also are presented in a useful, timeless fashion. Articles and book excerpts included in each title are selected if they contribute valuable, long-range ideas to the overall debate. And wherever possible, current information is enhanced with historical documents and other relevant materials. Thus, while individual titles are current in focus, every effort is made to ensure that they will not become quickly outdated. Books in the Current Controversies series will remain important resources for librarians, teachers, and students for many years.

In addition to keeping the titles focused and specific, great care is taken in the editorial format of each book in the series. Book introductions and chapter prefaces are offered to provide background material for readers. Chapters are organized around several key questions that are answered with diverse opinions representing all points on the political spectrum. Materials in each chapter include opinions in which authors clearly disagree as well as alternative opinions in which authors may agree on a broader issue but disagree on the possible solutions. In this way, the content of each volume in Current Controversies mirrors the mosaic of opinions encountered in society. Readers will quickly realize that there are many viable answers to these complex issues. By questioning each author's conclusions, students and casual readers can begin to develop the critical thinking skills so important to evaluating opinionated material.

Current Controversies is also ideal for controlled research. Each anthology in the series is composed of primary sources taken from a wide gamut of informational categories including periodicals, newspapers, books, US and foreign government documents, and the publications of private and public organizations. Readers will find factual support for reports, debates, and research papers covering all areas of important issues. In addition, an annotated table of contents, an index, a book and periodical bibliography, and a list of organizations to contact are included in each book to expedite further research.

Perhaps more than ever before in history, people are confronted with diverse and contradictory information. During the Persian Gulf War, for example, the public was not only treated to minute-to-minute coverage of the war, it was also inundated with critiques of the coverage and countless analyses of the factors motivating US involvement. Being able to sort through the plethora of opinions accompanying today's major issues, and to draw one's own conclusions, can be a complicated and frustrating struggle. It is the editors' hope that Current Controversies will help readers with this struggle.

Introduction

"Experts expect that the demand for apps will continue to grow almost indefinitely."

No technology has ever been adopted by the public as rapidly as smartphones and the apps, or software applications, that make them useful. The Apple App Store, the largest of the stores that offer mobile apps, opened in 2008. Less than five years later, in January 2013, an Apple press release announced there had been more than forty billion downloads of apps for the iPhone, iPad and iPod, not counting re-downloads and updates. Nearly twenty billion of them were in 2012 alone. Over 775,000 different apps are currently offered by that app store in 155 countries around the world. In addition, there are over seven hundred thousand apps in other stores for other mobile operating systems, including Android phones and more.

A recent survey by the Pew Research Center shows that two thirds of American adults connect to the Internet by a mobile device of some kind. According to one estimate, by 2016 there will be more mobile Internet devices than people on the planet (although of course this does not mean that everyone will have one, since many people own more than one device). It is widely agreed that mobile devices have had a significant impact on people's way of life.

The enthusiasm for mobile apps has created—and to some extent may have been created by—a fundamental change in the nature of the software industry. Formerly, software was sold in large units that enabled users to perform complex tasks such as word processing or photo editing. Such software is usually developed by teams of people working in big companies and takes months or years to create, which makes it expensive. Apps, on the other hand, can be created quickly by individuals. When big companies do produce apps, they create many separate ones instead of devoting a major share of their time and effort to a single software package. So apps can be sold for very little, often less than a dollar, or given away free as a venue for advertising. Because this leads people to buy a lot of them, many of the successful ones earn large sums of money for their developers. There is no longer as much demand for traditional software, since most computer users already have what they need, whereas new mobile apps are fun and appealing. Therefore, app development and marketing has become the focus of the software industry, creating hundreds of thousands of jobs in a range of activity commonly referred to as the "app economy."

Most experts expect that the demand for apps will continue to grow almost indefinitely, although there is strong disagreement about the future relative importance of mobile apps and websites. Certainly people will continue to want software that enables them to make full use of mobile devices. The technical differences between mobile apps and websites are likely to decrease as technology advances—for instance, some websites are able to detect whether the user has a small screen or a large one; the newest Web programming language, HTML5, offers both mobile apps and websites the ability to access some of mobile devices' hardware; and apps and Web-based tools alike are coming to rely more and more on remote storage of users' data on the Internet servers known as the cloud. However, the differences between the two involve more than technology.

A key difference between websites and apps is that websites can be made available by anyone to everyone, simply by uploading files to the Web for free viewing with a standard browser, whereas the distribution of apps is controlled. The creator of a mobile app cannot make it widely available unless it is accepted for inclusion in an app store (a process which in some cases can take months), and a user cannot obtain a mobile app without downloading it, often for a fee. Many people in the information technology field believe that the bulk of the material available to the public over the Internet should not be controlled, a philosophy known as the Open Web. On the other hand, some think that more and more users will prefer apps for specific purposes to browsing, which would be desirable from a software developers' standpoint because it would result in an increasing number of saleable products. Getting apps from an app store is quick, easy, and enjoyable, and for many people this may be an overriding factor. As Giacomo Mazzone, the head of institutional relations for the European Broadcasting Union, has predicted, "Instead of couch potatoes you'll have app-potatoes."

There is a possibility, however, that the vast number of mobile apps available may sooner or later be self-defeating with respect to their popularity. With over 775,000 apps available in a single app store, it is becoming difficult for people to locate and choose what they want. Some feel it is overwhelming. "When I got my first iPhone in late 2008, I couldn't wait to peruse the App Store for cool new games, neat productivity tools and quirky new social services," wrote Jenna Wortham in a *New York Times* blog on February 15, 2013. "Now the App Store just feels daunting . . . Who has the time to sift through that glut to uncover new gems?"

Moreover, some individuals have already installed hundreds of apps, making it hard to find what they want even on their own phones. Wortham said that she had 259 apps on hers. Most people find that they regularly use only a few of the apps they have installed, and each app takes up some of the device's memory; too many may slow its performance.

The ongoing proliferation of apps is creating other problems. Foremost among these is the issue of privacy, which is receiving increased attention as more and more people become aware that if they have apps on their phones their personal lives are not as private as they thought. Many apps collect and send personal information to third parties without the user's knowledge. Sometimes this is simply due to carelessness on the part of an app developer who has not given it enough thought; the software has access to address books, call logs, etc. that it does not need to retain, or does not need at all, and transmits it along with something else. Other times it is the user who has not bothered to restrict personal information on public websites such as Facebook that apps can obtain. But there are types of information that certain apps do need in order to function and that by their nature cannot always be restricted. Location data, for example, can be misused by recipients such as stalkers and advertisers, yet for some purposes users want their location to be known. The need to compromise between privacy and functionality is unavoidable.

These problems are not easy to resolve. There is a growing feeling that government regulations, or at least firm guidelines, should control what information apps are allowed to transmit. This is countered by the argument that regulation would prevent innovative apps with new capabilities from being created. Most people believe that any app should inform the user about what is being done with personal data and obtain his or her consent, but it is difficult to do this on a small screen, and not all users will take time to pay attention.

Another problem presented by apps is that of censorship. Do app developers have a constitutional right to free speech? Legally, no; constitutional restrictions apply to actions by the government, not private parties or organizations. There is no reason why an app store cannot choose what merchandise to offer, just as a bookstore or a clothing store can, and the time may come when there are so many apps on the market that selection will be necessary merely to ensure a manageable number to display. On the other hand, some apps deal with controversial ideas, and many people feel that it is wrong for sellers to censor ideas. They hold that apps should never be rejected on the basis of content unless it is something illegal such as obscenity or libel. However, these same people often argue for rejection of racist apps and others that certain groups find objectionable. The difficulty is that what is perceived as "objectionable" varies from group to group, and to avoid offending any group at all would mean suppressing the controversy between them.

The rapid takeover of the software industry by mobile apps could not have been predicted, and anything said in a book about it is almost sure to be outdated in some respects before the book has even been published. As Prue Duggan wrote in the blog *Backbase* in January 2013, "Everything happens faster in the digital jungle. . . . The mind boggling speed with which the terrain can change is nowhere more obvious than with the effortless, onward march of the app into our lives."

CHAPTER 1

Is There a Need for Oversight of the App Industry to Protect Privacy?

Overview: Lack of Privacy in Using Mobile Apps Is a Serious Problem

Al Franken

US Senator Al Franken is from Minnesota and he is the chairman of the Senate Judiciary Committee's Subcommittee on Privacy, Technology, and the Law.

To me, this subcommittee [US Senate Judiciary Committee's Subcommittee on Privacy, Technology, and the Law] is about addressing a fundamental shift that we've seen in the past 40 or 50 years in who has our information, and what they're doing with it.

When I was growing up, when people talked about protecting their privacy, they talked about protecting it from the government. They talked about unreasonable searches and seizures, about keeping the government out of our families and our bedrooms. They talked about "is the government trying to keep tabs on the books I read and the rallies I attend."

We still do have to protect ourselves from government abuses, and that's a big part of the digital privacy debate. But now we also have relationships with large corporations that are obtaining and storing increasingly large amounts of our information. And we've seen the growth of this whole other sphere of private entities whose entire purpose is to collect and aggregate information about each of us. . . .

Now, don't get me wrong, the existence of this business model is not a bad thing. In fact, I think it's usually a great thing. I love that I can use Google Maps—for free, no less, and the same for the app on my iPad that tells me the weather.

Al Franken, "Privacy, Technology, and Law: Protecting Mobile Privacy: Your Smartphones, Tablets, Cellphones and Your Privacy," U.S. Senate Subcommittee Hearing on Protecting Mobile Privacy, May 10, 2011.

But I think there's a balance we need to strike. And this means we're beginning to change the way we think about privacy to account for this massive shift of our personal information into the hands of the private sector—because the Fourth Amendment doesn't apply to corporations; the Freedom of Information Act doesn't apply to Silicon Valley.

And while business may do a lot of things better than the government, our government is at least by definition directly accountable to the American people.

Let me put it this way. If it came out that the DMV [Department of Motor Vehicles] was creating a detailed file on every single trip you'd taken in the past year—do you think they could go one whole week without answering a single question from a reporter? . . .

Consumers Have a Right to Control Data Collection

We have some protections here and there, but we're not even close to protecting all of the information that we need to. I believe that consumers have a fundamental right to know what data is being collected about them. I also believe that they have a right to decide whether they want to share that information, and with whom they want to share it and when. And I think we have those rights for all of our personal information.

Information on our mobile devices is not being protected in the way it should be.

My goal for this Subcommittee is to help members understand the benefits and privacy implications of new technology; to educate the public to raise awareness; and, if necessary, to legislate and make sure that our privacy protections are keeping up with our technology.

Now, today in this hearing, we're looking at a specific kind of really sensitive information that I don't think we're doing enough to protect. And that's data from mobile devices—smartphones, tablets, cell phones.

This technology gives us incredible benefits. It allows parents to see their kids and wish them goodnight—even when they are half a world apart. It allows a lost driver to get directions. And it allows emergency responders to locate a crash victim in a matter of seconds.

But the same information that allows those responders to locate us when we're in trouble is not necessarily information all of us want to share all the time with the entire world. And yet reports suggest that the information on our mobile devices is not being protected in the way it should be.

In December [2010], an investigation by the *Wall Street Journal* into 101 popular apps for iPhone and Android smartphones found that 47 of those apps—47—transmitted the smartphone's location to third party companies, and that most of them did this without their users' consent.

Three weeks ago, [April 2011] security researchers discovered that iPhones and iPads running Apple's latest operating system [iOS] were gathering information about users' location—up to 100 times a day—and storing that information on the phone or tablet and copying it to every computer that the device it synced to.

Soon after that, the American public also learned that both iPhones and Android [operating system] phones were automatically collecting certain location information from users' phones and sending it back to Apple and Google—even when people weren't using location applications.

In each of these cases, most users had no idea what was happening. And in many of these cases, once users learned about it, they had no way to stop it.

Breaches of Privacy Have Serious Consequences

These breaches of privacy can have real consequences for real people. A Justice Department report based on 2006 data shows that each year, over 26,000 adults are stalked through the use of GPS [Global Positioning System] devices, including GPS devices on mobile phones. That's from 2006—when there were a third as many smartphones as there are today.

Companies are free to disclose your location information and other sensitive information to almost anyone they please—without letting you know.

And when I sent a letter to Apple to ask the company about its logging of users' location, the first group to reach out to my office was the Minnesota Coalition for Battered Women. They asked: How can we help? Because we see case after case where a stalker or an abusive spouse has used the technology on mobile phones to stalk or harass their victims.

But it isn't just stalking. I think today's hearing will show that there is a range of harms that can come from privacy breaches. And there's also the simple fact that Americans want stronger protections for this information.

But as I've started to look into these issues in greater depth, I've realized that our federal laws do far too little to protect this information. Prosecutors bringing cases under the federal anti-hacking law often rely on breaches of privacy policies to make their case. But many mobile apps don't have privacy policies. And some policies are so long and complicated that they're almost universally dismissed without being read.

In fact, once the maker of a mobile app, a company like Apple or Google, or even your wireless company gets your location information, in many cases, under current federal law, these companies are free to disclose your location information and other sensitive information to almost anyone they please—without letting you know. And then the companies they share your information with can share and sell it to yet others—again, without letting you know.

This is a problem. It's a serious problem. And I think that's something the American people should be aware of, and I think it's a problem that we should be looking at. But before I turn it over to the distinguished Ranking Member, I just want to be clear that the answer to this problem is not ending location-based services. No one up here wants to stop Apple or Google from producing their products or doing the incredible things that you do. You guys are brilliant. When people think of the word "brilliant" they think of the people that founded and run your companies.

No. What today is about is trying to find a balance between all of those wonderful benefits and the public's right to privacy. And I for one think that's doable.

Legislation to Protect the Privacy of App Users Should Be Enacted by Congress

Justin Brookman

Justin Brookman is the director of consumer privacy at the Center for Democracy and Technology, a nonprofit public interest organization dedicated to preserving and promoting openness, innovation, and freedom on the decentralized Internet.

Mobile phones and tablets have exploded in popularity in recent years, and all evidence indicates that this trend will continue. Smartphone sales are expected to eclipse those of desktop and laptop computers combined in the next two years. However, mobile devices store and transmit a particularly personal set of data. These devices typically allow third parties to access personal information such as contact lists, pictures, browsing history, and identifying information more readily than in traditional internet web browsing. The devices also use and transmit information [such as] consumer's precise geolocation information as consumers travel from place to place.

At the same time, consumers have less control over their information on mobile devices than through traditional web browsing. While third parties, like ad networks, usually must use "cookies" to track users on the web, they often get access to unique—and unchangeable—unique device identifiers in the mobile space. While cookies can be deleted by savvy users, device identifiers are permanent, meaning data shared about your device can always be correlated with that device. As is the case with most consumer data, information generated by

Justin Brookman, "Testimony," U.S. Senate Subcommittee Hearing on Protecting Mobile Privacy, May 10, 2011.

mobile devices is for the most part not protected by current law and may be collected and shared without users' knowledge or consent.

Consumers interact with their mobile devices by running applications, or "apps" (i.e., programs designed to run on mobile devices). The mobile apps ecosystem is robust and offers an ever-increasing range of functionality from games, music, maps, instant messaging, email, metro schedules, and more. Mobile apps may be preinstalled on the device by the manufacturer or distributor, or users can download and install the programs themselves from their operating system's "apps store" (like iTunes or the Android Market), or a third-party store (like Amazon). App developers range from large, multinational corporations to individuals coding in their parents' basements. Generally speaking, we have seen a vibrant and creative app market develop for mobile devices. Unfortunately, it can be hard to know what information these apps have access to and with whom they are sharing it.

Recent studies of this flourishing apps data ecosystem have unearthed troubling findings. A recent survey indicated that of the top 340 free apps, only 19% contained a privacy policy *at all*. Last December [2010], the *Wall Street Journal* investigated the behavior of the 101 most popular mobile apps, finding that more than half transmitted the user's unique device ID to third parties without the user's consent. Forty-seven apps transmitted the phone's location. One popular music app, Pandora, sent users' age, gender, location and phone identifier to various ad networks. In sum, a small phone can leak a big amount of data.

Once an app has access to a user's data, there are usually no rules governing its disclosure, and no controls available to consumers to regain control of it. For the most part, once data leaves the phone, it is effectively "in the wild." It may be retained long after the moment of collection, and often long after the original service has been provided. App developers, advertisers, ad networks and platforms, analytics companies, and any number of other downstream players can share, sell, or unpredictably use data far into the future. Even insurance companies are eying data mined from online services for new predictive models. In short, today's mobile environment provides a gateway into an opaque and largely unregulated market for personal data.

> [Apps] may store detailed location and other customer information on the phone itself, which could then be accessed by government officials, . . . malicious hackers, or merely the person who finds your lost phone at Starbucks.

Location Data Is Sensitive Information

Location data is of particular concern. In recent years, the accuracy of location data has improved while the expense of calculating and obtaining it has declined. As a result, location-based services are an integral part of users' experiences and an increasingly important market for U.S. companies. Consumers like the convenience and relevance of location based services. Location data can be used guide you to the closest coffee shop or help you navigate an unfamiliar neighborhood. Your location can be leveraged to connect you with coupons or deals in your immediate vicinity. And new, innovative, and useful services are introduced daily.

People generally carry their mobile devices wherever they go, making it possible for location data be collected everywhere, at any time, and potentially without prompting. Understandably, many find the use of location data without clear transparency and control troubling. Research shows that people value their location privacy and are less comfortable sharing their location with strangers than with acquaintances, and want granular control over their location information. Indeed, location data is especially sensitive information that can be used to decipher revealing facts or put people at physical risk. Location information could disclose visits to sensitive destinations, like medical clinics, courts and political rallies. Access to location can also be used in stalking and domestic violence. Finally as an increasing number of minors carry location-capable cell phones and devices, location privacy may become a child safety matter as well.

There are also questions and concerns about the collection, usage, and storage of data by mobile platform providers such as Apple and Google. Because in many instances, these companies are the ones actually calculating your location (based on comparing the WiFi access points in range of your device with known databases), they may receive extremely detailed information about consumer activity, considerably more so than traditional computer operating systems. Although these companies typically assert that data they receive from consumers is anonymized and used merely to build out their databases of access points, these limitations are self-imposed. Furthermore, these platforms may store detailed location and other customer information on the phone itself, which could then be accessed by government officials, potentially without a warrant, malicious hackers, or merely the person who finds your lost phone at Starbucks.

Mobile devices and the services they enable provide consumers with great benefit. But it is imperative that Congress provide a clear policy framework to protect users' privacy and trust. CDT [Center for Democracy and Technology] strongly supports privacy legislation that implements the full range of Fair Information Practice Principles (FIPPs) across all consumer data and provides enhanced protections for sensitive information, such as precise geolocation, including enhanced, affirmative opt-in consent.

Unfortunately, today's legal protections fall far short. . . .

A Data Privacy Law Is Needed

Given that the default rule for most consumer data—including sensitive location data—is merely that companies cannot make affirmative misstatements about the use of that data, CDT strongly supports the enactment of a uniform set of baseline rules for personal information collected both online and offline. Modern data flows often involve the collection and use of data derived and combined from both online and offline sources, and the rights of consumers and obligations of companies with respect to consumer data should apply to both as well. The mobile device space implicates many different kinds of data in a complicated ecosystem. Cramming more notices onto small screens is alone insufficient. We need a data privacy law that incentivizes and requires companies to provide clear and conspicuous notice to consumers about the use of their information and provides for meaningful control of that information. Moreover, companies should collect only as much personal information as necessary, be clear about with whom they're sharing information, and expunge information after it is no longer needed.

The Fair Information Practice Principles should be the foundation of any comprehensive privacy framework. FIPPs have been embodied to varying degrees in the Privacy Act, Fair Credit Reporting Act, and other sectoral federal privacy laws that govern commercial uses of information online and offline. The most recent formulation of the FIPPs by the Department of Homeland Security offers a robust set of modernized principles that should serve as the foundation for any discussion of consumer privacy legislation. Those principles are:

- Transparency

- Purpose Specification

- Use Limitation

- Data Minimization

- Data Accuracy

- Individual Participation

- Security

- Accountability

For particularly sensitive data, such as health information, financial information, information about religion or sexuality, and—most relevant here—precise geolocation data, a legislative framework should provide for enhanced application of the Fair Information Practice Principles, including for affirmative opt-in consent for the collection and/or transfer of such information. Consumers understandably have greater concerns about the use and storage of such information, and the law should err against presuming a consumer's assent to share such information with others.

Furthermore, as noted above, the laws governing government access to consumer data should be modernized to require a warrant to access sensitive location information.

Congress Is Considering Legislation to Ban Cyberstalking Apps

Richard Lardner

Richard Lardner is a writer for the Associated Press.

For around $50, a jealous wife or husband can download software that can continuously track the whereabouts of a spouse better than any private detective. It's frighteningly easy and effective in an age when nearly everyone carries a cellphone that can record every moment of a person's physical movements. But it soon might be illegal.

The Senate Judiciary Committee was expected Thursday [December 2012] to approve legislation that would close a legal loophole that allows so-called cyberstalking apps to operate secretly on a cellphone and transmit the user's location information without a person's knowledge.

The bill, sponsored by Sen. Al Franken, D-Minn., would update laws passed years before wireless technology revolutionized communications. Telephone companies currently are barred from disclosing to businesses the locations of people when they make a traditional phone call. But there's no such prohibition when communicating over the Internet. If a mobile device sends an email, links to a website or launches an app, the precise location of the phone can be passed to advertisers, marketers and others without the user's permission.

Stealth Phone Spy Software

The ambiguity has created a niche for companies like Retina Software, which makes ePhoneTracker and describes it as "stealth phone spy software."

"Suspect your spouse is cheating?" the company's website says. "Don't break the bank by hiring a private investigator."

An emailed statement from Retina Software said the program is for the lawful monitoring of a cellphone that the purchaser of the software owns and has a right to monitor. If there is evidence the customer doesn't own the phone, the account is closed, the company said. The program is not intended or marketed for malicious purposes, the statement said.

But Franken and supporters of his bill said there is no way to ensure the rules are followed. These programs can be installed in moments, perhaps while the cellphone's actual owner is sleeping or in the shower. The apps operate invisibly to the cellphone's user. They can silently record text messages, call logs, physical locations and visits to websites. All the information is relayed to an email address chosen by the installer.

Even if people do discover the software is installed on their phones, they often don't know what to do about it, said Rick Mislan, a professor at the Rochester Institute of Technology who specializes in mobile security and forensics. "Law enforcement usually won't help them because they've got bigger fish to fry," he said.

Companies would face a criminal penalty if they knowingly operate an app with the intent to facilitate stalking.

Victim's advocacy groups said Franken's bill is a common-sense step to curb stalking and domestic violence by weakening a tool that gives one person power over another.

"It's really, really troubling that an industry would see an opportunity to make money off of strengthening someone's opportunity to control and threaten another individual," said Karen Jarmoc, executive director of the Connecticut Coalition Against Domestic Violence.

Domestic Abusers Can Trace Victims

A domestic violence case in St. Louis County, Minn., helped persuade Franken to introduce his bill. A woman had entered a county building to meet with her advocate when she received a text message from her abuser asking her why she was there, according to congressional testimony delivered last year by the National Network to End Domestic Violence. Frightened, she and her advocate went to the local courthouse to file for a protective order. She got another text demanding to know why she was at the courthouse. They later determined her abuser was tracing her movements with an app that had been placed on her cellphone. The woman was not identified by name in the congressional testimony.

Franken's proposal would make companies subject to civil liability if they fail to secure permission before obtaining location information from a person's cellphone and sharing it with anyone else. They also would be liable if they fail to tell a user no later than seven days after the service begins that the program is running on their phone. Companies would face a criminal penalty if they knowingly operate an app with the intent to facilitate stalking.

The bill includes an exception to the permission requirement for parents who want to place tracking software on the cellphones of minor children without them being aware it is there.

An organization representing software companies opposes Franken's bill because it said the user consent requirement would curb innovation in the private sector without adequately addressing the problem of cyberstalking. Voluntary but enforceable codes of conduct for the industry are more effective methods for increasing transparency and consumer confidence, said David LeDuc, senior director for public policy at the Software & Information Industry Association.

Some Misuses of Mobile Apps Can Be Dealt with by Consumer Protection Laws

Jessica Rich

Jessica Rich is the deputy director of the Bureau of Consumer Protection at the Federal Trade Commission.

New technology can bring tremendous benefits to consumers, but it also can present new concerns and provide a platform for old frauds to resurface. Mobile technology is no different. Although there are no special laws applicable to mobile marketing that the FTC [Federal Trade Commission] enforces, the FTC's core consumer protection law—Section 5 of the FTC Act—prohibits unfair or deceptive practices in the mobile arena. This law applies to marketing in all media, whether traditional print, telephone, television, desktop computer, or mobile device.

For more than a decade, the Commission has explored mobile and wireless issues, starting in 2000 when the agency hosted a two-day workshop studying emerging wireless Internet and data technologies and the privacy, security, and consumer protection issues they raise. In addition, in November 2006, the Commission held a three-day technology forum that prominently featured mobile issues. Shortly thereafter, the Commission hosted two Town Hall meetings to explore the use of radio frequency identification (RFID) technology, and its integration into mobile devices as a contactless payment system. And in 2008, the Commission held a two-day forum examining consumer protection issues in the mobile sphere,

Jessica Rich, "Testimony," U.S. Senate Subcommittee Hearing on Protecting Mobile Privacy, May 10, 2011.

including issues relating to ringtones, games, chat services, mobile coupons, and location-based services.

More recently, the agency has invested in new technologies to provide its investigators and attorneys with the necessary tools to monitor and respond to the growth of the mobile marketplace. For example, the Commission has established a mobile technology laboratory, akin to the Commission's long-standing Internet investigative laboratory, containing a variety of smartphones utilizing different platforms and carriers, as well as software and equipment that permit FTC investigators to collect and preserve evidence and conduct research into a wide range of mobile issues, including those related to consumer privacy.

Applying the FTC Act to the Mobile Arena

Law enforcement is the Commission's most visible and effective tool for fighting online threats, including those in the mobile marketplace. As described below, the FTC has brought four recent cases that illustrate how Section 5 applies to the mobile arena, including unsolicited text messages and the privacy and security of data collected on mobile devices.

In August 2010, the Commission charged Reverb Communications, Inc., a public relations agency hired to promote video games, with deceptively endorsing mobile gaming applications in the iTunes store. The company allegedly posted positive reviews of gaming apps using account names that gave the impression the reviews had been submitted by disinterested consumers when they were, in actuality, posted by Reverb employees. In addition, the Commission charged that Reverb failed to disclose that it often received a percentage of the sales of each game. The Commission charged that the disguised reviews were deceptive under Section 5, because knowing the connection between the reviewers and the game developers would have been material to consumers reviewing the iTunes posts in deciding whether or not to purchase the games. In settling the allegations, the company agreed to an order prohibiting it from publishing reviews of any products or services unless it discloses a material connection, when one exists, between the company and the product. The *Reverb* settlement demonstrates that the FTC's well-settled truth-in-advertising principles apply to new forms of mobile marketing.

In February [2011], the Commission filed its first law enforcement action against a sender of unsolicited text messages and obtained a temporary restraining order suspending the defendant's challenged operations. The FTC alleged that Philip Flora used 32 pre-paid cell phones to send over 5 million unsolicited text messages—almost a million a week—to the mobile phones of U.S. consumers. Many consumers who received Flora's text messages—which typically advertised questionable mortgage loan modification or debt relief services—had to pay a per-message fee each time they received a message. Many others found that Flora's text messages caused them to exceed the number of messages included in their mobile service plans, thereby causing some consumers to incur additional charges on their monthly bill. The Commission charged Flora with the unfair practice of sending unsolicited text messages and with deceptively claiming an affiliation with the federal government in connection with the loan modification service advertised in the text messages.

Mobile technology presents unique and heightened privacy and security concerns.

The FTC has also taken action against companies that fail to protect the privacy and security of consumer information. Two recent cases highlight the FTC's efforts to challenge deceptive claims that undermine consumers' privacy choices in the mobile marketplace.

First, the Commission's recent case against Google alleges that the company deceived consumers by using information collected from Gmail users to generate and populate a new social network, Google Buzz. The Commission charged that Gmail users' associations with their frequent email contacts became public without the users' consent. As part of the Commission's proposed settlement order, Google must protect the privacy of all of its customers—including mobile users. For example, if Google changes a product or service in a way that makes consumer information more widely available, it must seek affirmative express consent to such a change. This provision applies to *any* data collected from or about consumers, including mobile data. In addition, the order requires Google to implement a comprehensive privacy program and conduct independent audits every other year for the next 20 years.

The rush of on-the-go use, coupled with the small screens of most mobile devices, makes it ... unlikely that consumers will read detailed privacy disclosures.

Second, in the Commission's case against social networking service Twitter, the FTC charged that serious lapses in the company's data security allowed hackers to obtain unauthorized administrative control of Twitter. As a result, hackers had access to private "tweets" and non-public user information—including users' mobile phone numbers—and took over user accounts, among them, those of then-President-elect [Barack] Obama and [media magnate] Rupert Murdoch. The Commission's order, which applies to Twitter's collection and use of consumer data, including through mobile devices or applications, prohibits misrepresentations about the extent to which Twitter protects the privacy of communications, requires Twitter to maintain reasonable security, and mandates independent, comprehensive audits of Twitter's security practices.

These are just two recent examples of cases involving mobile privacy issues, but the Commission's enforcement efforts are ongoing. Staff has a number of active investigations into privacy issues associated with mobile devices, including children's privacy.

Mobile Privacy Policy Initiatives

As noted, the rapid growth of mobile technologies has led to the development of many new business models involving mobile services. On the one hand, these innovations provide valuable benefits to both businesses and consumers. On the other hand, they facilitate unprecedented levels of data collection, which are often invisible to consumers.

The Commission recognizes that mobile technology presents unique and heightened privacy and security concerns. In the complicated mobile ecosystem, a single mobile device can facilitate data collection and sharing among many entities, including wireless providers, mobile operating system providers, handset manufacturers, application developers, analytics companies, and advertisers. And, unlike other types of technology, mobile devices are typically personal to the user, almost always carried by the user and switched-on. From capturing consumers' precise location to their interactions with email, social networks, and apps, companies can use a mobile device to collect data over time and "reveal the habits and patterns that mark the distinction between a day in the life and a way of life." Further, the rush of on-the-go use, coupled with the small screens of most mobile devices, makes it even more unlikely that consumers will read detailed privacy disclosures.

In recent months, news reports have highlighted the virtually ubiquitous data collection by smartphones and their apps. Researchers announced that Apple has been collecting geolocation data through its mobile devices over time, and storing unencrypted data files containing this information on consumers' computers and mobile devices. The *Wall Street Journal* has documented numerous companies gaining access to detailed information—such as age, gender, precise location, and the unique identifiers associated with a particular mobile device—that can then be used to track and predict consumers' every move. Not surprisingly, recent surveys indicate that consumers are concerned. For example, a recent Nielsen study found that a majority of smartphone app users worry about their privacy when it comes to sharing their location through a mobile device.

Companies should . . . obtain affirmative express consent before collecting or sharing sensitive information such as precise geolocation data.

Privacy Roundtables

The Commission has been considering these and related issues in connection with its "Exploring Privacy" Roundtable series. In late 2009 and early 2010, the Commission held three roundtables to examine how changes in the marketplace have affected consumer privacy and whether current privacy laws and frameworks have kept pace with these changes. During the second roundtable, one panel in particular focused on the privacy implications of mobile technology, addressing the complexity of data collection through mobile devices; the extent and nature of the data collection, particularly with respect to geolocation data; and the adequacy of privacy disclosures on mobile devices.

Based on the information received through the roundtable process, staff drafted a preliminary report (Staff Report) proposing a new privacy framework consisting of three main recommendations, each of which is applicable to mobile technology. First, staff recommends that companies should adopt a "privacy by design" approach by building privacy protections into their everyday business practices, such as not collecting or retaining more data than they need to provide a requested service or transaction. Thus, for example, if an app is providing traffic and weather information to a consumer, it does not need to collect call logs or contact lists from the consumer's device. Further, although the app may need location information, the app developer should carefully consider how long the location information should be retained to provide the requested service.

Second, staff recommends that companies should provide simpler and more streamlined privacy choices to consumers. This means that all companies involved in data collection and sharing through mobile devices—carriers, handset manufacturers, operating system providers, app developers, and advertisers—should work together to provide these choices and to ensure that they are understandable and accessible on the small screen. As stated in the Staff Report, companies should also obtain affirmative express consent before collecting or sharing sensitive information such as precise geolocation data.

Third, the Staff Report proposed a number of measures that companies should take to make their data practices more transparent to consumers, including improving disclosures to consumers about information practices. Again, because of the small size of the device, a key question staff posed in the report is how companies can create effective notices and present them on mobile devices.

After releasing the Staff Report, staff received 452 public comments on its proposed framework, a number of which implicate mobile privacy issues specifically. FTC staff is analyzing the comments and will take them in consideration in preparing a final report for release later this year [2011].

The Commission is committed to protecting consumers' privacy in the mobile sphere by bringing enforcement where appropriate and by working with industry and consumer groups to develop workable solutions that protect consumers while allowing innovation in this growing marketplace.

The Federal Trade Commission Has Found that Apps Invade the Privacy of Children and Teens

Federal Trade Commission

The Federal Trade Commission (FTC) is an independent agency of the US government responsible for consumer protection and the elimination and prevention of anti-competitive business practices.

The Federal Trade Commission [FTC] today [February 2012] issued a staff report showing the results of a survey of mobile apps for children. The survey shows that neither the app stores nor the app developers provide the information parents need to determine what data is being collected from their children, how it is being shared, or who will have access to it.

"At the FTC, one of our highest priorities is protecting children's privacy, and parents deserve the tools to help them do that," said FTC Chairman Jon Leibowitz. "Companies that operate in the mobile marketplace provide great benefits, but they must step up to the plate and provide easily accessible, basic information, so that parents can make informed decisions about the apps their kids use. Right now, it is almost impossible to figure out which apps collect data and what they do with it. The kids app ecosystem needs to wake up, and we want to work collaboratively with the industry to help ensure parents have the information they need."

According to the FTC report, *Mobile Apps for Kids: Current Privacy Disclosures Are Disappointing*, in 2008, smartphone us-

Federal Trade Commission, "FTC Report Raises Privacy Questions About Mobile Applications for Children," February 16, 2012.

ers could choose from about 600 available apps. Today there are more than 500,000 apps in the Apple App Store and 380,000 in the Android Market. "Consumers have downloaded these apps more than 28 billion times, and young children and teens are increasingly embracing smartphone technology for entertainment and educational purposes."

The report says the survey focused on the largest stores, the Apple App Store and the Android Market, and evaluated the types of apps offered to children, the disclosures provided to users, interactive features such as connectivity with social media, and the ratings and parental controls offered for such apps.

More should be done to identify the best way to convey data practices in plain language and in easily accessible ways on the small screens of mobile devices.

Lack of Information About Data Collection

The report notes that mobile apps can capture a broad range of user information from a mobile device automatically, including the user's precise geolocation, phone number, list of contacts, call logs, unique identifiers, and other information stored on the device. At the same time, "the report highlights the lack of information available to parents prior to downloading mobile apps for their children, and calls on industry to provide greater transparency about their data practices."

While there was a diverse pool of kids apps created by hundreds of different developers, there was almost no information about the data collection and sharing on the Apple App store promotion pages and little information beyond general permission statements on the Android Market promotion pages. "In most instances, staff was unable to determine from the information on the app store page or the developer's landing page whether an app collected any data, let alone the type of data collected, the purpose for such collection, and who . . . obtained access to such data."

The report recommends:

- All members of the "kids app ecosystem"—the stores, developers and third parties providing services—should play an active role in providing key information to parents.

- App developers should provide data practices information in simple and short disclosures. They also should disclose whether the app connects with social media, and whether it contains ads. Third parties that collect data also should disclose their privacy practices.

- App stores also should take responsibility for ensuring that parents have basic information. "As gatekeepers of the app marketplace, the app stores should do more." The report notes that the stores provide architecture for sharing pricing and category data, and should be able to provide a way for developers to provide information about their data collection and sharing practices.

The report notes that more should be done to identify the best way to convey data practices in plain language and in easily accessible ways on the small screens of mobile devices. The agency will host a public workshop in 2012, in connection with its efforts to update the FTC's "Dot Com Disclosure" guide, about how to provide effective online disclosures. "One of the topics that will be addressed is mobile privacy disclosures, including how they can be short, effective, and accessible to consumers on small screens."

The FTC enforces the Children's Online Privacy Protection Rule. The Rule requires operators of online services, including interactive mobile apps, to provide notice and get parental consent prior to collecting information from children under 13. The report says in the next 6 months, FTC staff will conduct an additional review to determine whether some mobile apps were violating COPPA [Children's Online Privacy Protection Act].

The Federal Trade Commission works for consumers to prevent fraudulent, deceptive, and unfair business practices and to provide information to help spot, stop, and avoid them. The FTC enters complaints into Consumer Sentinel, a secure, online database available to more than 2,000 civil and criminal law enforcement agencies in the U.S. and abroad. The FTC's website provides free information on a variety of consumer topics.

Mobile App Developers Should Observe Privacy Practices Recommended by the Government

Kamala Harris

Kamala Harris is the attorney general of the California Department of Justice.

Mobile devices are integral to modern life and their use is growing rapidly. Today, 85 percent of American adults have a cell phone, 45 percent a smart phone [mobile phone with an operating system that allows installation of apps, as distinguished from a phone that has only built-in features], 61 percent a laptop, 25 percent a tablet computer, and 18 percent an e-book reader. Over half of adult cell phone owners use the Internet on their phones, twice the rate in 2009. And nearly one third of cell owners report that their phone is the primary, or only, way they access the Internet.

The ever-expanding capabilities of mobile devices have created an exploding market for applications (apps) that allow us not just to read books, play games, listen to music, and take photos and videos, but also to monitor our heart rate, start the car remotely on a dark night, find a nearby restaurant, and pay for purchases on-the-spot. Recent reports estimate that there are more than a million apps available on the primary mobile platforms, and more than 1,600 new apps are added daily.

Clearly, many consumers find value in mobile apps and are eager to try new ones as they are released. But many of these same consumers are also concerned about privacy. A re-

Kamala Harris, "Privacy on the Go: Recommendations for the Mobile Ecosystem," California Department of Justice, January 2013, pp. 3–6.

cent study found that more than half of mobile app users had uninstalled or decided not to install an app because of concerns about its privacy practices. Addressing these concerns is essential to protect consumers and to foster trust and confidence in this market.

The mobile app industry is in a relatively early development stage, with developers focusing on getting new products to market as quickly as possible, sometimes without adequate consideration of privacy.

Mobile Privacy Issues

Our smart phones and other mobile devices are pocket computers. They now have the power and functionality of desktop computers—and the privacy and security risks inherent to the Internet. Like our desktop and laptop computers, our mobile devices may contain, or are capable of accessing, large amounts of personal information: contact information of our friends and associates, family photos and videos, and our web browsing history, among other details. And like personal computers, smart phones, and other mobile devices are targets for malware [malicious software] and spyware.

These always-on, always-on-us devices pose additional privacy challenges that are unique to the mobile space. Mobile devices may store types of user information not usually found on personal computers, such as telephone call logs, text messages, and a history of our location. Mobile devices and apps are also leading to new forms and combinations of user and device-related data that may pose new risks to users' privacy and security.

Another challenge is the devices' small screens, which make the effective communication of privacy practices and user choices difficult. Furthermore, although the app economy is thriving, the mobile app industry is in a relatively early development stage, with developers focusing on getting new products to market as quickly as possible, sometimes without adequate consideration of privacy. Recent studies, for example, have found that many mobile apps did not provide users with privacy policy statements at all. This represents not just a failure in transparency, but it also suggests a lack of attention to the apps' privacy practices.

In an important step to strengthen the privacy protections for users of mobile applications, the California Attorney General in early 2012 announced a Joint Statement of Principles, endorsed by the companies whose platforms comprise the majority of the mobile app market (Amazon, Apple, Facebook, Google, Hewlett-Packard, Microsoft, and Research In Motion). The principles are intended to ensure that mobile apps comply with applicable privacy laws such as the California Online Privacy Protection Act, and include the conspicuous posting of a privacy policy by mobile apps when required by law, a means to make the policy available from the app platform before downloading, a way for users to report non-compliant apps to the platform provider, a process to respond to such reports, and a pledge to further work with the Attorney General on best practices for mobile privacy. As of October 2012, all the app store companies who joined the agreement reported that they had implemented the principles.

The agreement with the platform providers has already had an impact on privacy practices. A June 2012 study found that the percentage of the most popular apps with some form of access to a privacy policy improved significantly since their similar study in September 2011. In just eight months, free apps on the Apple App Store platform with a privacy policy doubled, from 40 percent to 84 percent, and those on the Google Play platform increased from 70 percent to 76 percent.

Recommended Practices

The Attorney General is committed to increasing compliance with California's privacy laws. In July 2012, the Attorney General created the Privacy Enforcement and Protection Unit, with the mission of protecting the inalienable right to privacy conferred by the California Constitution. The Privacy Unit enforces state and federal privacy laws, and develops programs to educate consumers and businesses on privacy rights and best practices. *Privacy on the Go* is part of the effort to encourage businesses to adopt privacy best practices.

Several respected organizations have recently issued privacy principles and policies for the mobile industry. The shared themes of these sets of principles have informed our recommended practices: transparency about data practices, limits on the collection and retention of data, meaningful choices for users, security, and accountability of all industry actors for privacy.

We offer these privacy practice recommendations to assist the mobile ecosystem in the ongoing efforts to develop privacy standards. Our hope is that privacy-respectful practices such as those we are recommending here will be adopted by app developers and others, enabling consumers to make informed choices from the vast array of mobile apps while maintaining the level of privacy control they desire.

Our recommendations, which in many places offer greater protection than afforded by existing law, are intended to encourage all players in the mobile marketplace to consider privacy implications *at the outset* of the design process. They are also intended to encourage the alignment of architectural and functional decisions with the widely accepted Fair Information Practice Principles (FIPPs). The FIPPs form the basis for many privacy codes and laws in different parts of the world, including the federal Privacy Act of 1974 and the similar California Information Practices Act of 1977.

Like many actors in the mobile ecosystem, the Attorney General is also participating in the multi-stakeholder process facilitated by the National Telecommunications and Information Administration (NTIA) to develop an enforceable code of conduct on mobile app transparency. While our recommendations engage a broader range of mobile privacy issues than the NTIA is expected to address at this time, we hope that this document will be useful in the ongoing NTIA process.

Surprise Minimization

The basic approach recommended here is to minimize surprises to users from unexpected privacy practices. An obvious way to avoid such unpleasant surprises is to avoid collecting personally indentifiable data from users that are not needed for an app's basic functionality.

Another important step is to make an app's general privacy policy easy to understand and readily available *before* a mobile app is downloaded. It is widely recognized, however, that in order to make meaningful choices, consumers need clearer, shorter notices of certain privacy practices. This is particularly true in the small-screen mobile environment. Our recommended approach is to supplement the legally required general privacy policy with enhanced measures to alert users and give them control over data practices that are not related to an app's basic functionality or that involve sensitive information.

Such enhanced notice and control might be provided through "special notices," delivered in context and just-in-time. For example, operating systems that use location data deliver a notice just before collecting the data and give users an opportunity to allow or prevent the practice.

Another way to achieve the same end is to make readily available from within an app both a short privacy statement highlighting potentially unexpected practices, and privacy controls that allow users to make, review, and change their privacy choices.

Shared Accountability

We are addressing these initial recommendations primarily to app developers, but we include some recommendations to other actors in the ecosystem.

Protecting consumer privacy is a team sport. The decisions and actions of many players, operating individually and jointly, determine privacy outcomes for users. Hardware manufacturers, operating system developers, mobile telecommunications carriers, advertising networks, and mobile app developers all play a part, and their collaboration is crucial to enabling consumers to enjoy mobile apps without having to sacrifice their privacy.

By offering consumers greater transparency and control over how their information is collected and used in the mobile ecosystem, the industry will build the trust that is critical for the app market to flourish.

The Software Industry, Not Congress, Should Develop Privacy Guidelines for Mobile Apps

Mark MacCarthy

Mark MacCarthy is vice president for government affairs at the Software & Information Industry Association, a trade group for the software and digital content industry.

Mobile software applications have become an innovative and wildly popular tool for entertainment, business and education because they can be used on the go. Moreover, these apps can use location information to create targeted services with innovative benefits and features that most users highly value. The dramatic growth in the use of these new software tools is a tribute to the value they provide to users and to the innovative skills and responsibility of the app developers who have built this market.

Most mobile app developers are behaving responsibly in their collection and use of personal information. Still, it is clear that continued growth and innovation in the mobile marketplace is dependent on maintaining consumer confidence in privacy protection.

For this reason, the Software & Information Industry Association [SIIA] is committed to helping the mobile app community come together to create best practices for privacy. While legislators already have started to investigate the issue, we believe industry—not Congress—is best positioned to develop effective practices that ensure consumer confidence.

Mobile Privacy: No Need to Legislate

Mobile privacy became a major issue in Congress this spring [2011] when the Senate held back-to-back hearings on consumer privacy in mobile platforms—one in the Commerce Committee and another in the Judiciary Committee. In June, Sens. Al Franken, D-Minn., and Richard Blumenthal, D-Conn., introduced the 2011 Location Privacy Protection Act to mandate consumer control over the collection and use of location information from mobile devices.

Legislation that develops privacy rules specifically for mobile devices is premature, especially when the industry already is moving forward. The Future of Privacy Forum [FPF], a Washington think tank, has developed an application privacy working group, of which SIIA is a member. Through this group, we are bringing to bear the expertise of our member companies to develop voluntary guidelines that will spread best practices to all participants in the industry. In addition, the FPF project website, supported by SIIA and others, makes available a variety of tools to help app developers manage issues of data collection and use.

These efforts make it clear that the mobile app industry does not need government regulation to move us in the direction of providing a trusted environment for our users. We can do it ourselves, and the first step is straightforward guidelines from the industry for responsible collection and use of mobile data.

Legislation that develops privacy rules specifically for mobile devices is premature, especially when the industry already is moving forward.

Disclosure: A Critical Next Step

Responsible behavior by mobile app developers is already a feature of the marketplace. Numerous companies, including many members of SIIA, provide mobile software for business, consumer and educational uses. These mobile uses are a natural extension of the core services these companies provide to their clients. In this business-to-business or business-to-school context, transparency disclosures and information about the sharing and use of mobile information are handled as part of contractual negotiations and ongoing business relationships.

In order to foster an environment of confidence and trust, however, it is critical that all mobile app developers describe and disclose their information handling practices when they collect and use personal information.

The best methods for disclosing information handling practices are the subject of intense discussion within the app development community and at the Future of Privacy Forum. And as the *Washington Post* recently reported, a number of industry efforts are under way for companies to display their privacy policies in a way that overcomes the problems associated with a small screen and complicated legal disclaimers.

Guidelines Before Government Intervention

Most mobile app developers are careful and accountable in their use of personal information. But it is critical that the mobile app industry develop guidelines that clearly express these best practices and ensure that they are widely diffused throughout the industry. The creation of these industrywide guidelines—not legislation—is the logical next step.

Legislation, however well-intended, could cut short the growth of this nascent and largely American-based industry, and could stifle the innovation and creativity that has truly changed the way consumers work, play and interact.

SIIA joined the Future of Privacy Forum's application privacy working group out of the conviction that the industry does not need government to force us to provide a trusted environment for our users. We can and should do it ourselves.

Government Privacy Restrictions on Apps Would Lead to Decline of the App Economy

Jamie Tucker

Jamie Tucker is a partner in the Washington office of law firm Akin Gump Strauss Hauer & Feld.

Facebook Inc.'s $1 billion acquisition of Instagram Inc. [in April 2012] made headlines both for the size of the deal and for the many users of the popular mobile photo-sharing application who pulled it from their smartphones, citing concerns about the privacy of their data.

This rapid consumer reaction, and the slower but more significant legislative activity related to mobile privacy issues, raises the possibility that American technological innovation, particularly in the realm of mobile application development, could be headed for a train wreck as federal policymakers focus their attention on mobile device privacy and raise the specter of regulations that could unintentionally stifle innovation and kill jobs.

Reaction to the Facebook-Instagram deal provides a chance to look at several legal and regulatory initiatives that could have a significant impact on the future development of mobile applications software used in smartphones and other devices. These are a $20 billion and growing piece of our economy, one of the few sectors that generated expansion and job creation through the depths of the Great Recession, though that could be quashed—and investors could suffer—if the spate of pending legislation is passed without serious examination of its unintended consequences.

Mobile analytics company Carrier IQ Inc. gained notoriety in December [2011] when a programmer discovered that its software, embedded in 141 million phones, was tracking and recording keystrokes, including text messages, phone numbers and Web searches. More recently, popular social networks such as Path, Yelp Inc., Twitter Inc. and Facebook have drawn scrutiny for accessing, storing or transmitting users' address books without their knowledge.

These incidents highlight the need for privacy enhancements in the rapidly evolving mobile app space. Before imposing new restrictions that could slam the brakes on this economic engine, regulators in Congress and at the Federal Trade Commission [FTC] must carefully consider what drives this industry and the consequences that new regulations could have for companies—tech and traditional—as well as for average smartphone and tablet users.

Potential Consequences of Regulations

The growth of mobile apps has been explosive by any metric, providing a needed spark to the economy. Apps generate economic activity through app purchases, advertising within apps, or "appvertising," and facilitation of consumer spending through apps. According to a recent estimate by AppNation Inc. and Rubinson Partners Inc., the "app economy" generated nearly $20 billion in revenue in 2011, a figure they expect to quadruple by 2015.

While that revenue growth is staggering, let's also consider jobs, a top issue for voters and Washington policymakers. Roughly 1 million apps have been created for the iPhone, iPad and Android platforms [devices with different operating systems], and more are on the way. Every new app represents new jobs for programmers, advertisers and retailers. The

AppNation-Rubinson report estimates that 466,000 jobs are linked to the app economy, a sector that only emerged in mid-2008. During that 3 ½ year span, the economy as a whole lost 4 million jobs.

These new jobs are spread across the country. Seventy-five percent were created outside of tech-heavy California, in New York, Dallas, Washington, Chicago and Atlanta. A robust, job-creating sector sprang up, virtually overnight, due to strong demand for the increasingly sophisticated and consumer-friendly apps being developed by American innovators.

Yet expansion in this space is at risk of slowing due to the collision of two trends. Privacy concerns led regulators and policymakers to train their sights on mobile apps, and many apps are developed by small businesses incapable of complying with complex legislation or agency rules.

Every time a mobile app is found to be secretly tracking GPS [Global Positioning System] locations, copying address books or recording browsing histories, regulators are emboldened. Rather than punish just the offenders, some in Congress advocate imposing one-size-fits-all restrictions on the entire app economy. Five bills have been introduced, each bestowing new rulemaking authority upon the FTC to dictate how mobile apps operate. The bipartisan sponsors of key legislation include Sen. Jay Rockefeller, D-W.Va.; Reps. Joe Barton, R-Texas, and Edward Markey, D-Mass.; Sens. Al Franken, D-Minn., and Richard Blumenthal, D-Conn.; Rep. Jason Chaffetz, R-Utah; and Sen. Ron Wyden, D-Ore. (Markey introduced a second bill in the aftermath of the Carrier IQ incident.)

The motivation guiding these proposals is laudable, but the methods threaten to upend the mobile app sector by adding new compliance costs and injecting the threat of crippling financial penalties. Rockefeller's Do-Not-Track Online Act of 2011 authorizes civil penalties up to $15 million, for instance, and Markey's draft legislation allows for private lawsuits in addition to any civil penalties. Further, it imposes burdensome filing requirements with two separate federal agencies, the FTC and the Federal Communications Commission.

> *If burdensome, inflexible regulations were to be imposed on the mobile app sector ... development of apps could stall, causing a decline in the app economy as rapid as its initial acceleration.*

Small Businesses Could Not Meet Regulatory Requirements

Also, most app innovators are ill equipped to make the changes being discussed by Congress. According to the Association for Competitive Technology, 88% of the top-selling 500 apps are developed by small businesses, most of which have fewer than 10 employees. Few of these microbusinesses have legal departments capable of counseling on new regulatory obligations. The threat of additional compliance costs, as well as financial penalties, may impede future growth of this industry and the jobs it creates.

The Carrier IQ and Path incidents have exposed privacy risks that must be addressed, but they must be addressed in a thoughtful manner. The app industry should be given a chance to establish self-regulatory guidelines—with government and consumer input—that protect users and preserve businesses' ability to innovate. For instance, the [Barack] Obama administration's privacy initiative, launched Feb. 23, [2012] offers a model for addressing mobile privacy concerns through multistakeholder working groups that set voluntary codes of conduct. On Feb. 29, the Commerce Department indicated that mobile transparency may be the first topic tackled by the multistakeholder group. And on Feb. 27, a worldwide association of mobile operators known as the GSMA published new guidelines for protecting app users by increasing transparency, choice and control. Before heavy-handed legislation or regulations are imposed, voluntary, flexible and collaborative efforts such as these should be given a chance.

Some observers are quick to dismiss the prospects for mobile privacy legislation, given the inability of Congress to pass even noncontroversial legislation. Interested parties should still follow this debate closely.

Sufficient risks and potentially broad impacts remain considerable. If burdensome, inflexible regulations were to be imposed on the mobile app sector, the consequences could be far-reaching. Development of apps could stall, causing a decline in the app economy as rapid as its initial acceleration. Average users would be deprived of the next generation of innovations on their smartphones and tablets, and the U.S. economy could take a hit in direct and indirect job creation in a vital industry-leading sector.

Facebook Users Should Be Aware of How Data They Make Public May Be Used by Apps

John Brownlee

John Brownlee is deputy editor of the daily news website Cult of Mac, and has also written for many major print publications.

It was the flush end of a pleasurably hot day—85 degrees in March—and we were all sipping bitter cocktails out in my friend's backyard, which was both his smoking room, beer garden, viticetum, opossum parlor and barbecue pit. I was enjoying the warm dusk with a group of six of my best friends, all of whom seemed interested, except for my girlfriend . . . who immediately grimaced. . . .

"He's become obsessed with this app. It's *creepy.*"

I sputtered, I nevered, and I denied it, but it was true. I *had* become obsessed with Girls Around Me, an app that perfectly distills many of the most worrying issues related to social networking, privacy and the rise of the smartphone into a perfect case study that anyone can understand.

It's an app that can be interpreted many ways. It is as innocent as it is insidious; it is just as likely to be reacted to with laughter as it is with tears; it is as much of a novelty as it has the potential to be used a tool for rapists and stalkers.

And more than anything, it's a wake-up call about privacy.

The only way to really explain Girls Around Me to people is to load it up and show them how it works, so I did. I placed my iPhone on the table in front of everyone, and opened the app.

The splash screen elicited laughter all around. It's such a bitmap paean to the tackiest and most self-parodying of baller "culture"; it might as well be an app [fictional character] Tom Haverford slapped together in *Parks And Recreation* [TV show]. But it does, at a glance, sum up what Girls Around Me is all about: a radar overlaid on top of a Google Map, out of which throbs numerous holographic women posing like pole dancers in a perpetual state of undress.

"Okay, so here's the way the app works," I explained to my friends.

App Stalks Women Without Their Knowledge

Girls Around Me is a standard geolocation based maps app, similar to any other app that attempts to alert you to things of interest in your immediate vicinity: whether it be parties, clubs, deals, or what have you. When you load it up, the first thing Girls Around Me does is figure out where you are and load up a Google Map centered around your location. The rest of the interface is very simple: in the top left corner, there's a button that looks like a radar display, at the right corner, there's a fuel meter (used to fund the app's freemium model), and on the bottom left is a button that allows you to specify between whether you're interested in women, men or both.

It's when you push the radar button that Girls Around Me does what it says on the tin. I pressed the button for my friends. Immediately, Girls Around Me went into radar mode, and after just a few seconds, the map around us was filled with pictures of girls who were in the neighborhood. Since I was showing off the app on a Saturday night, there were dozens of girls out on the town in our local area.

"Wait . . . what? Are these girls prostitutes?" one of my friends asked, which given the Matrix-like silhouettes posing on the splash screen was a pretty good question.

"Oh, no," I replied. "These are just regular girls. See this girl? Her name's Zoe. She lives on the same street as me and Brittany. She works at a coffee shop, and I'm pretty sure she doesn't moonlight picking up tricks."

"How does it know where these girls are? Do you know all these girls? Is it plucking data from your address book or something?" another friend asked.

Most privacy settings on social networks default to share everything with everyone, and since most people never change those ... well, they end up getting sucked up into apps like this.

Data Obtained from Public Facebook Profiles

"Not at all. These are all girls with publicly visible Facebook profiles who have checked into these locations recently using Foursquare. Girls Around Me then shows you a map where all the girls are in your area trackable by Foursquare area. If there's more than one girl at a location, you see the number of girls there in a red bubble. Click on that, and you can see pictures of all the girls who are at that location at any given time. The pictures you are seeing are their social network profile pictures."

"Okay, so they *know* that their data can be used like this for anyone to see? They're okay with it?"

"Probably not, actually. The settings determining how visible your Facebook and Foursquare data is are complicated, and tend to be meaningless to people who don't really understand issues about privacy," I explained. "Most privacy settings on social networks default to share everything with everyone, and since most people never change those ... well, they end up getting sucked up into apps like this."

"But they know they've checked in, right?"

"Again, not necessarily. Foursquare lets you check other people into a location. If you get checked into Foursquare by a friend without your knowledge and have a publicly visible Facebook profile, you could end up in here." (*Update: Apparently, I wasn't correct about this. Foursquare does NOT allow you to check other people in with you without their knowledge; I was confusing Foursquare for Facebook, which does offer this functionality.*)

Facebook Users Are Unaware of How Their Data Is Being Used

One of my less computer-affable friends actually went pale, and kept on shooting her boyfriend looks for assurance. A Linux [a computer operating system] aficionado who was the only person in our group without a Facebook account (and one of the few people I'd ever met who actually endorsed Diaspora [a "Privacy Aware Open Source Social Network"]), the look he returned was one of comical smugness.

"But wait! It gets worse!" I said, ramping things up.

"So let's say I'm a bro, looking to go out for a night on the town and pick someone up. Let's say I'm going to the Independent around the corner, and checking it out ahead of time, I really like the look of this girl Zoe—she looks like a girl I might want to try to get with tonight—so I tap her picture for more information, see what I can find out about her."

I tapped on Zoe. Girls Around Me quickly loaded up a fullscreen render of her Facebook profile picture. The app then told me where Zoe had last been seen (The Independent) and when (15 minutes ago). A big green button at the bottom reading "Photos & Messaging" just begged to be tapped, and when I did, I was whisked away to Zoe's Facebook profile.

"Okay, so here's Zoe. Most of her information is visible, so I now know her full name. I can see at a glance that she's single, that she is 24, that she went to Stoneham High School and Bunker Hill Community College, that she likes to travel, that her favorite book is *Gone With The Wind* and her favorite musician is Tori Amos, and that she's a liberal. I can see the names of her family and friends. I can see her birthday."

"All of that is visible on Facebook?" one of the other girls in our group asked.

"More, depending on how your privacy settings are configured! For example, I can also look at Zoe's pictures."

I tapped on the photo album, and a collection of hundreds of publicly visible photos loaded up. I quickly browsed them.

"Okay, so it looks like Zoe is my kind of girl. From her photo albums, I can see that she likes to party, and given the number of guys she takes photos with at bars and clubs at night, I can deduce that she's frisky when she's drunk, and her favorite drink is a frosty margarita. She appears to have recently been in Rome. Also, since her photo album contains pictures she took at the beach, I now know what Zoe looks like in a bikini . . . which, as it happens, is pretty damn good."

My girlfriend scowled at me. I assured her Zoe in a bikini was no comparison, and moved on.

"So now I know everything to know about Zoe. I know where she is. I know what she looks like, both clothed and mostly disrobed. I know her full name, her parents' full names, her brother's full name. I know what she likes to drink. I know where she went to school. I know what she likes and dislikes. All I need to do now is go down to the Independent, ask her if she remembers me from Stoneham High, ask her how her brother Mike is doing, buy her a frosty margarita, and start waxing eloquently about that beautiful summer I spent in Roma."

Throughout this demonstration, my group of friends had been split pretty evenly along gender lines in their reactions. Across the board, the men either looked amused or (in the case of my beardo Diaspora friend) philosophically pleased with themselves about their existing opinions about social networking. The women, on the other hand, looked sick and horrified.

It was at this point, though, that the tendrils of the girls' unease—their deeply empathic sense of someone being *unsafe*—seemed to creep through the entire group.

On the surface, it looks like a hook-up app . . . for potential stalkers and date rapists, but all that Girls Around Me is really doing is using public APIs from Google Maps, Facebook and Foursquare.

"And if that doesn't work on Zoe," I concluded, consulting the app one last time. "There are—let's see—*nine* other girls at the Independent tonight."

Often times, a writer uses tricks and exaggerations to convey to a reader the spirit—if not the precise truth—of what occurred. I just want to make clear that when I say that one of my friends was actually on the verge of tears, you understand that this is *not* such a trick. She was horrified to the point of crying.

"How can Apple let people download an app like this?" she asked. "And have you *written* about this?"

Such Uses Do Not Violate Any Policies

In answer to the first question, I replied that as sleazy as this app seemed, Girls Around Me wasn't actually doing anything wrong. Sure, on the surface, it looks like a hook-up app like Grindr for potential stalkers and date rapists, but all that Girls Around Me is really doing is using public APIs [application programming interfaces] from Google Maps, Facebook and Foursquare and mashing them all up together, so you could see who had checked-in at locations in your area, and learn more about them. Moreover, the girls (and men!) shown in Girls Around Me all had the power to opt out of this information being visible to strangers, but whether out of igno-rance, apathy or laziness, they had all neglected to do so. This was all public information. Nothing Girls Around Me does violates any of Apple's policies.

In fact, Girls Around Me wasn't even the real problem.

"It's not, really, that we're all horrified by what this app *does*, is it?" I asked, finishing my drink. "It's that we're all hor-rified by how exposed these girls are, and how exposed ser-vices like Facebook and Foursquare *let* them be without their knowledge."

But I didn't have an easy answer ready for my friend's last question. I'd been playing with the app for almost two months. Why hadn't I written about it? None of the answers made me look good.

Part of it was because, like many tech professionals, I had taken for granted that people understood that their Facebook profiles and Foursquare data were publicly visible unless they explicitly said otherwise . . . and like my beardo Diaspora friend, I secretly believed that people who were exposed this way on the Internet without their knowledge were foolish.

That made Girls Around Me a funny curio, a titillating novelty app, the kind of thing you pulled out with your bud-dies at the bar to laugh about . . . and maybe secretly wish had been around when you were younger and single and trying to pull some action. And if I'd written a post about it a month ago, it would have probably been from that angle. The head-line might well have been: "No More Sausage Fests With Girls Around Me [Humor]."

This is an app you should download to teach the people you care about that privacy issues are real.

It was in just this spirit that I'd shown off the app to my friends in the first place. It was getting late, we were all drunk or on the verge of getting there, and it had been a perfect day.

It would have been so nice to finish things with a laugh. But now, as six intelligent, sophisticated friends from a variety of backgrounds surrounded me—some looking sick, some looking angry, and some with genuine fear in their faces—I didn't think Girls Around Me was so funny. It had cast a pall across a beautiful day, and it had made people I loved feel scared . . . not just for the people *they* loved, but for complete strangers.

Social Network Privacy Issues Are Real

So I'm writing about it now. Not because Girls Around Me is an evil app that should be pulled from the iOS [Apple operating system] App Store, or because the company that makes it—Moscow-based i-Free—is filled with villains. I still don't believe that there's anything wrong with what this app is doing, and the guys at i-Free are super nice, and certainly don't mean for this app to be anything beyond a diversion. So, the reason I'm writing about Girls Around Me is because I finally know what to say about it, and what it means in the greater picture.

Girls Around Me isn't an app you should use to pick up girls, or guys for that matter. This is an app you should download to teach the people you care about that privacy issues are real, that social networks like Facebook and Foursquare expose you and the ones you love, and that if you do not know exactly how much you are sharing, you are as easily preyed upon as if you were naked. I can think of no better way to get a person to realize that they should understand their Facebook privacy settings then pulling out this app.

That's why I hope you'll go download Girls Around Me on your iPhone or iPad. It's free to download. Show it to someone. Give them the same demo I gave to my friends. Then, when they ask how it's done and how they can prevent an app like Girls Around Me from tracking them, educate them about privacy.

CHAPTER 2

Should Controversial Mobile Apps Be Taken Off the Market?

App stores: Gatekeepers, or Censors of the Mobile Web?

Doug Gross

Doug Gross is a reporter for CNN.

It's been framed as a debate between Web freedom and the freedom from stumbling upon potentially offensive content.

In recent weeks, several companies have been forced to grapple with sexually explicit images appearing in their popular mobile apps. Such images, a small fraction of the apps' user-generated content, place these companies at risk for being banned from portals such as Apple's App Store, where millions of people gain access to the mobile Web.

But some observers see something more at play here.

"In this debate, some may focus on freedom and others may focus on the harm of adult content, but what's really happening here is the crystallization of the power of platform providers—Apple, Google, Microsoft and even Amazon," said James McQuivey, a tech-industry analyst at Forrester Research.

"These companies are free to set their own standards in the interest of their customers, even if that means that they 'censor' some content in service of other content."

The most high-profile episode happened last week [January 2013] after Twitter unveiled Vine, a mobile app that lets users shoot and post looping, six-second video clips. It took off with users even quicker than folks at the social network expected.

And, as such, Vine quickly became a victim of what has colloquially become known as the Internet's Rule 34—"If it exists, there is porn on it."

Racy video clips, including one that accidentally popped up in the app's "Editor's Picks" section, led Twitter to make it harder for users to seek out adult content using hashtags like #porn and #naked. Before that, Apple had removed Vine from its "Editor's Choice" section in its App Store, the only place Vine is currently available.

On Wednesday [February 6, 2013], the age rating for Vine in the App Store was raised from 12+ to 17+, roughly the equivalent of a movie's rating being changed from PG-13 to the more restrictive R. To download the app users must tap a window vowing they are over 17, although there is no verification system.

A week earlier [January 2013], Apple banned 500px, a photo-sharing app, because it said users could easily access sexual images. The app's creators argued that 500px's only adult images were a small number of artistic nude photos.

Apple eventually restored the app, but only after 500px agreed to raise its age rating from 4+ to 17+.

In the wake of those two moves, Tumblr, the widely popular blogging platform that includes some porn among its roughly 92 million blogs, similarly reclassified itself with the 17+ tag.

All of a sudden, we're putting big decisions about what we can and can't see into the hands of for-profit companies.

Companies Make More Censorship Decisions than Governments

The significance here, some say, is that the Web is increasingly becoming a mobile one. In the United States, 45% of people owned a smartphone last year, which is more than owned an older-style "feature phone." That's not to mention the millions more worldwide using tablets and other devices as their main entry point onto the Internet.

"If iPad Nation were a country, it would be in the top 10 largest countries in the world with more than 100 million citizens," McQuivey said. "This is more evidence that platforms like these companies are becoming more important than governments in some respect."

If those mobile-device owners aren't using Apple products, they probably use Google's Android system, or Microsoft's or BlackBerry's.

So, all of a sudden, we're putting big decisions about what we can and can't see into the hands of for-profit companies. That has some observers worried.

Yes, virtually all mobile devices have a Web browser that lets the user get to the rest of the Internet's content, app store or not. But a single tap of a finger is a lot easier than thumbing a Web address into a tiny browser.

"There are some advantages to being an application," said Parker Higgins of the Electronic Frontier Foundation, a group that promotes digital rights. "To deny those advantages to certain kinds of unpopular speech doesn't seem appropriate."

Apple ends up at the center of these conversations, both due to its prominence in the tech world and the famously tight controls it keeps on its "walled garden" of data.

The company continues to argue for an experience that the late CEO [chief executive officer] Steve Jobs once described as "(f)reedom from programs that steal your private data. Freedom from programs that trash your battery. Freedom from porn."

Decisions About What to Ban Are Not Always Fair

But critics, including some app developers, argue Apple's garden isn't policed in a fair way. Why, for example, was 500px banned, but not the more prominent Tumblr? Has Apple leaned on Twitter, which activists have lauded for its devotion to Web freedoms, to change Vine's 12+ age rating?

"I'm not saying that Apple is being malicious—they have a billion apps in that store," Higgins said. "It's not that they're doing the wrong thing on purpose. It's just too big a job for anyone to be expected to regulate all that."

He notes, though, that the bans haven't always been about porn or spam or inefficient apps.

Last year, an app that would have pinpointed the location of U.S. drone strikes in the Middle East was rejected multiple times. And two years ago, Pulitzer Prize-winning cartoonist Mark Fiore's app was rejected because it "contains content that ridicules public officials." (It was eventually approved after public outcry.)

"That's pretty plainly political speech," Higgins said of the apps.

Apple did not reply to questions submitted for this article.

But the company makes no bones about having tight controls on the App Store.

Companies are making decisions that, rhetoric aside, are never wholly about the end users' rights or concerns.

"If it sounds like we're control freaks, well, maybe it's because we're so committed to our users and making sure they have a quality experience with our products," the company writes in its App Store review guidelines.

Google has guidelines for its Google Play mobile store. But they tend to be looser than Apple's. The Android system also lets apps from outside stores be loaded onto the phones and tablets that use it.

Google also did not reply to a request for comment.

That, of course, opens up the user to the possibilities Jobs mentioned—call it Android's wild, and potentially dangerous, jungle outside of Apple's aforementioned garden.

Regardless of the specifics of their approaches, though, these companies are making decisions that, rhetoric aside, are never wholly about the end users' rights or concerns.

"Their job is to make money by cultivating a base of customers," said Forrester's McQuivey. "If they deem some content will harm that relationship, they are free to ban it.

"As a result, traditional thoughts about government censorship or control are no longer relevant—no matter how upsetting that will be to people on either side of this particular debate."

Sellers Have a Right to Decline to Sell Apps They Find Objectionable

Theodore Kruczek

Theodore Kruczek is a student at the US Air Force Academy.

To start, I do not own anything made by Apple. I do not like the censorship of the App store. I have never been a fan of the way the company has an "i" in front of everything they sell. So clearly, I am not a Mac-lover. With that being said, I would like to explain why I support Apple in censoring their App Store and why you should too.

For those of you who are unfamiliar with the matter, let me explain the censorship. On Apple's popular iTouch, iPhone, and iPad, all applications, dubbed "Apps", are downloaded from a central location called the App Store. Companies (or individuals) are able to submit their Apps to the App Store for review by Apple. They must meet strict guidelines involving efficiency, functionality, privacy settings, and a "no porn" policy. This has led to many popular Apps being removed for failure to comply. Most recently, Apple's policy on not supporting flash has resulted in many Apps being nothing more than a scrollable.pdf version of a website.

With these overbearing policies that reminded me of Nintendo's censorship of games, I was a strong critic of Apple. Although they offer one of, if not the best, user interfaces—mainly because all of the programs have to comply with the standard—I was simply unhappy with the way they limit creativity. Apple has always been well known for their popularity amongst the artists, graphic designers, and film editors, which only seemed more ironic to me that they would limit what people can do with their creative talents. I did, do, and will always support a free and open-source internet. The internet provides a great medium for expression and learning, and I don't want to see it limited.

It should be the right of every company to operate in the way it feels necessary to achieve the goals they have.

After all of that, you would expect me to have to be against Apple on this. Today my mind was changed due to a posted conversation between Steve Jobs [the chief executive officer (CEO) of Apple] and a Gawker Media reporter. First, I want to say my respect for Steve Jobs couldn't be higher knowing that he took the time to defend his company against an inebriated writer at two in the morning. He explained that Apple is censoring the Apps to ensure the user experience that it wants for its company. Apple is not pushing for universal censorship of the internet or computers, only on the Apple platform that they publish. He argued that it should be the right of every company to operate in the way it feels necessary to achieve the goals they have. One of the amusing ones he mentioned was "freedom from porn". That is really a non-issue to me, but to some I imagine it could be a big concern and Apple is choosing to cater to them.

Support Companies' Right to Censor

You should support them in their attempts to build the Apple platform they want. If you don't like it—get something else. I love using Linux, but hate the effort needed to do simple tasks sometimes. I wait hopeful that Ubuntu will overtake Windows, but until then I am gonna stick to using what allows the most flexibility and reliability—Windows 7. At the same time, I am going to hope that my friends who want the control Apple offers on its content, will have that as an option.

Competition is what drives development. If we kick Apple out of the equation because they have a radical idea, then we could potentially be stuck in a 1D computer realm where everything is what it is and if it isn't what you wanted—O well.

Do I like the censorship—no way! Do some people like it—yep. So let us all stop bashing Steve Jobs for doing what he is proving works for many people. If we don't like his method, let's buy something else or go open-source until he finds it better to cater to us. If he doesn't, he will either go broke while we are enjoying our alternative, or he will remain rich while we get what we really wanted. Either way, we should get what we want and let him do his thing. If you love Apple but are upset by the recent changes in censorship—nothing tells the CEO that better than a discontinuing of purchases.

Apps that Are Offensive to Gays Should Be Rejected by App Stores

Truth Wins Out

Truth Wins Out is a nonprofit think tank and educational organization that debunks the ex-gay myth and provides accurate information about the lives of lesbian, gay, bisexual, and transgender (LGBT) people.

Exodus International, the notorious "ex-gay" organization, has just released an iPhone app that, according to its website, is "designed to be a useful resource for men, women, parents, students, and ministry leaders." The Exodus website further boasts that its app received a 4+ rating from Apple, meaning that it contains "no objectionable content."

No objectionable content? We beg to differ. Exodus' message is hateful and bigoted. They claim to offer "freedom from homosexuality through the power of Jesus Christ" and use scare tactics, misinformation, stereotypes and distortions of LGBT [lesbian, gay, bisexual, and transgender] life to recruit clients. They endorse the use of so-called "reparative therapy" to "change" the sexual orientation of their clients, despite the fact that this form of "therapy" has been rejected by every major professional medical organization including the American Psychological Association, the American Medical Association, and the American Counseling Association. But reparative therapy isn't just bad medicine—it's also very damaging to the self-esteem and mental health of its victims.

This new iPhone app is the latest move in Exodus' dangerous new strategy of targeting youth. In light of the recent wave of LGBT youth suicides, this tactic is particularly galling as it creates, legitimizes, and fuels the ostracism of LGBT youth by their families. According to a [2009] study published in the *Journal of the American Academy of Pediatrics*, LGBT teens who experienced negative feedback from their family were 8 times more likely to have attempted suicide, 6 times as vulnerable to severe depression, and 3 times more likely to use drugs.

Apple doesn't allow racist or anti-Semitic apps in its app store, yet it [gave] the green light to an app targeting vulnerable LGBT youth.

Apple's app guidelines, released last September [2010], detailed rules on how the company decides what can and cannot be sold through its store: "Any app that is defamatory, offensive, mean-spirited, or likely to place the targeted individual or group in harms way will be rejected," the company states.

Apple doesn't allow racist or anti-Semitic apps in its app store, yet it is giving the green light to an app targeting vulnerable LGBT youth with the message that their sexual orientation is a "sin that will make your heart sick" and a "counterfeit." This is a double standard that has the potential for devastating consequences.

Apple needs to be told, loud and clear, that this is unacceptable. Stand with Truth Wins Out—demand that the iTunes store stop supporting homophobia and remove the Exodus app.

[The following petition appeared on Change.org.]

To: [Apple executives]

I am writing today to ask you to remove the Exodus International application from the iTunes store.

Apple has long been a friend of the LGBT community, opposing California's Proposition 8, removing the anti-gay Manhattan Declaration iPhone app, and earning a 100% score from the Human Rights Campaign's Corporate Equality Index.

That's why I am shocked that this same company has given the green light to an app from a notoriously anti-gay organization like Exodus International that uses scare tactics, misinformation, stereotypes and distortions of LGBT life to recruit clients, endorses the use of so-called "reparative therapy" to "change" the sexual orientation of their clients (despite the fact that this form of "therapy" has been roundly condemned by every major professional medical organization), and targets vulnerable, suicide-prone LGBT youth with the message that their sexual orientation is a "sin that will make your heart sick" and a "counterfeit," contributing to and legitimizing the ostracism of these youth from their families.

Apple's app guidelines released in September last year detailed rules on how the company decides what can and cannot be sold through its store: "Any app that is defamatory, offensive, mean-spirited, or likely to place the targeted individual or group in harms way will be rejected," the company states.

Apple would never allow a racist or anti-Semitic app to be sold in the iTunes store, and for good reason. Apple's approval of the anti-gay Exodus International app represents a double standard for the LGBT community with potentially devastating consequences for our youth. This is unacceptable, and I urge you to take a strong stance against homophobia by removing this dangerous "ex-gay" iPhone app from the store.

Victory

Tech giant Apple faced considerable pressure to pull an app from its App Store, produced by Exodus International, that advocated "curing" gay people of their sexual orientation. After 150,000 emails from Change.org members, and considerable pressure from the group Truth Wins Out, Apple pulled the app, agreeing that it was offensive and in violation of their editorial standards. John Becker, Director of Communications and Development with Truth Wins Out, thanked Change.org members for helping push Apple on this issue. "Truth Wins Out was honored to have the support of more than 150,000 Change.org members, who helped send a message to Apple that 'ex-gay' therapy is dangerous, harmful, damaging, and has no place on the iTunes platform," said Becker. "This is really a testament to how the power of online organizing can be harnessed to advance social change and confront homophobia."

Campaign Apps Should Not Be Censored by Stores on the Basis of Political Bias

Mitch Wagner

Mitch Wagner is a technology journalist and social media strategist.

A Republican Congressional candidate says Apple blocked distribution of his campaign app through the iPhone App Store, one of several politically conservative apps that Apple censored while allowing more liberal equivalents to get published.

Ari David, a conservative running in Santa Monica, Calif., says Apple blocked his app because it was "defamatory" of the incumbent for that seat, powerful Democrat Henry Waxman, according to a May 15 [2010] statement on David's Web site.

The post lists statements that Apple found defamatory, criticizing Waxman's stand on Cap & Trade legislation, cuts to Medicare spending, opposition to missile funding, and that Waxman "tried to strangle family farms with insane Soviet-style regulation."

I spoke with David Sunday [May 2010]. He said since posting that statement on his Web site, his staff researched the history of Apple screening political apps in the App Store, and found a liberal bias.

Apple rejected an application called iSlam Muhammad that criticized the Quran, while permitting BibleThumper, which similarly criticizes the Christian Bible, David said.

From the App Store description of BibleThumper:

Mitch Wagner, "Apple Censors Republican Congressional Candidate," *ComputerWorld*, May 24, 2010. Reproduced by permission.

This is the perfect Atheist bible companion! Next time one of those bible thumpers starts proselytizing, you will be able to answer in kind with the juiciest quotes straight from the holy bible. Included are a selection of the most funny, irrational & strange quotes from the bible.

Apple also permitted iChe, an application celebrating Che Guevera [Argentine Marxist revolutionary], according to David.

Earlier, Apple rejected an app by Pulitzer-Prize-winning political cartoonist Mark Fiore, although Apple later relented and now offers the NewsToons app in the App Store. The NewsToons app included political satire against President [Barack] Obama, among other figures.

With the iPhone becoming the standard for mobile applications, it is wrong for them to stifle expression of certain ideas.

I asked David whether Apple has a right to block apps—even block them in a politically biased fashion—given that Apple owns the App Store. "Absolutely," David said. "There's nothing necessarily legally wrong with it, just as there's also nothing wrong with me in a political season revealing to the world what's wrong with my opponent."

He added, "I don't have a Constitutional right to an iPhone application, but they don't have a right to keep me from talking."

Legalities aside, I asked David if he thinks it's right for Apple to filter political apps. He said, "The way I look at it, iPhone applications are becoming somewhat of a de facto standard. Similar to the way Hare Krishnas [religious movement] are allowed to give out flowers and literature at the airport, even if the airport is privately run in partnership with the public, with the iPhone becoming the standard for mobile applications, it is wrong for them to stifle expression of certain ideas with the world through the portal."

He denied that the app's statements about Waxman are defamatory. "It was not defamatory, it was true, famously true. Waxman is famous for getting healthcare passed, and promoting the Cap & Trade bill. If we're just saying things that are known facts within the media, for Apple to call that speech defamatory is looking at it from a very biased perspective."

Apple can continue to block porn and other graphic content, but it should explicitly allow political speech, which most definitely includes "defamation" of public figures.

David's experience is just the latest example of problems with App Store filtering. The process is broken. Apple can take several routes to fix it.

Apple could throw the iPhone open to all developers, as the Mac is now. In this scenario, Apple could keep the App Store as is, for apps getting the Apple seal of approval, but also allow users to install apps from anywhere. That would be the ideal solution; after all, it's the user's phone, the user paid for it, and should be able to install whatever apps he wants to install. But I don't see that as likely; it violates Apple's central business model for the iPhone.

Another option would be to filter apps for technical reasons, but not for content. If your app is a security risk or unstable, then it gets blocked, but everything else goes. That's unlikely too; Steve Jobs [chief executive officer of Apple] reportedly wants to keep the App Store family-friendly. Civil libertarians chafe at those kinds of restrictions, but they're hardly new, they go back at least a century in America, and we as a society have managed to work around those restrictions to have free discourse on other subjects.

Still, even if the App Store continues to block adult content, it needs to grow up. Apple can continue to block porn and other graphic content, but it should explicitly allow political speech, which most definitely includes "defamation" of public figures. Stop treating your customers like babies, Apple, you're better than that.

(Also, would it kill you to answer e-mail every once in a while? As usual, Apple did not respond to a request for comment on this blog. And it's not just me, Apple is notoriously loath to talk to bloggers and journalists.)

Apps Should Not Be Censored by Stores for Politically-Sensitive Content

John Paul Titlow

John Paul Titlow writes for the tech blog ReadWrite, *focusing on the future of music and entertainment, the ongoing online copyright wars, and Apple.*

I was hoping to wake up to different headlines this morning [September 2012]. Something along the line of "Apple Apologizes, Accepts Drone+ iPhone App" would have sufficed. Alas, last week's news remains a stubborn reality: Apple thinks that an app highlighting publicly available data about war is "objectionable" and refuses to allow it into the App Store. The event illustrates one of Apple's very worst tendencies.

The app in question is Drone+, a project by NYU [New York University] grad student Josh Begley that displays an interactive map of recent U.S. drone strikes in Pakistan. After two prior rejections by Apple for reasons having to do with utility and design, the app was nixed a third time for containing "objectionable content."

The decision was a bit of a head-scratcher, considering that a very similar feature was already included in the *Guardian*'s iPhone app and that scattered information about U.S. drone strikes can be found throughout dozens of news apps that are readily available on the App Store.

Quality Control vs. Censorship

To be fair, this decision is not as troubling as it would be if Apple were a government or a publisher in the traditional sense. Still, it's a new kind of gatekeeper, and it holds the keys to a platform used by millions of people around the world. While not as horrifyingly Orwellian [referring to the fictional totalitarian society described in a novel by George Orwell] as it could be, the fact that the biggest company in U.S. history makes decisions about which content is too "objectionable" for its customers is unsettling.

Why does content that effectively agitates for one government to be overthrown make the cut, while content that may make another government look bad (depending on one's own perspective) doesn't?

Apple has every right to maintain strict guidelines as to what can go into the App Store. This is what keeps the experience so smooth and beloved by consumers. If a developer submits an app with crummy functionality or a confusing UI [user interface], Apple should reject it. But if a developer submits an app with politically sensitive words or pictures, so long as it's not obscene (pornography in the Apple Store is a debate for another day), in violation of copyright law or libelous, the company should back off.

This is a lesson Apple should have learned in 2010, when it rejected an app submitted by a Pulitzer Prize-winning political cartoonist [Mark Fiore] because it ridiculed public figures. That, of course, is something newspapers have done freely for centuries, and the blatant disregard for free speech resulted in a PR [public relations] headache for Apple.

In that case, the company reversed its stance and accepted the app. It should do the same for Drone+. Then it should tweak its submission policies to get out of the business of censorship.

Twenty-Five Billion Apps Later, Things Have Changed

Things have changed since Apple launched the App Store in 2008. For one thing, the platform has become wildly successful and iOS [Apple operating system] device sales now make up a huge majority of Apple's record-breaking profits. More than 25 billion apps have been downloaded from the App Store.

Meanwhile, we've seen social media and mobile technology play a crucial role in political uprisings in the Arab world and beyond. Those events have been sparked by unrest due to economic and political conditions but, in case after case, networked communications have stoked the flames.

Last year in Syria, antigovernment activists began using an iPhone app to disseminate news, maps, photos and videos about the conflict in a country that doesn't exactly rank highly for its press freedom. Mobile tech in the hands of Syrian dissidents proved enough of a nuisance that the government banned the iPhone in late 2011, presumably to quash content that the regime found, um, objectionable.

This example raises a few questions. First, why are pins on a map more objectionable than photos and video clips from a war zone? Why does content that effectively agitates for one government to be overthrown make the cut, while content that may make another government look bad (depending on one's own perspective) doesn't? Is Apple taking sides in international conflicts? Perhaps more disturbing is the notion that, were Apple to apply these standards consistently, apps like the one used by Syrian dissidents—and perhaps some news apps—would be barred from the App Store as well.

Apple Risks Losing Consumer Trust—For What?

Censorship doesn't help consumers, but it doesn't do Apple any favors either. Apple is at the top of the food chain when it comes to tech companies. Its profits are soaring. Consumers' mouths are watering for the upcoming iPhone 5, iPad Mini and whatever other polished, connected gadget the company may launch in the foreseeable future. People will stand in line for those products whether or not Apple accepts or rejects any particular app.

Even so, the company would be unwise to take the trust of its customers for granted. People get queasy when they perceive censorship, no matter where they stand politically. A series of news stories highlighting Apple's insensitivity to freedom of expression could eat away at public trust, even in a brand as bullet-proof as Apple's.

Consumers' lives are increasingly connected, ever more deeply embedded in mobile devices and social networks. These are pretty radical changes, and they're happening more quickly than many people (not to mention industries and governments) can respond. Some consumers are already beginning to grow uncomfortable with Facebook's privacy policies, Google's targeted advertising, and other cases in which, whether justified or not, technology starts to feel a little creepy. Twitter takes protecting privacy and free speech very seriously, and even if most users don't notice or care yet, that stance will serve the company well as social media continues to part and parcel our daily lives.

Further, there's no business rationale for blocking apps like this. Does it really degrade the iPhone or iPad experience if people can download an app that shows them where U.S. drones are killing civilians in Pakistan? People who care about that information will download the app, and those who don't will continue playing Angry Birds and reading Flipboard.

Apple is a stickler when it comes to design, user experience, legal concerns, and overall quality. It has a legitimate right to protect its brand by rejecting adult-oriented apps. But when it comes to news, commentary and hard data, Apple has more to lose than to gain from rejecting content it doesn't like.

Some Retailers Censor Apps Too Inconsistently to Retain Public Confidence

Sarah Weinman

Sarah Weinman is the news editor at Publisher's Marketplace and has written articles for many major national print and online publications.

For as long as Apple has had its best-selling iPhones and iPads on the market they've taken an aggressive stance on what type of content is appropriate for the devices. As CEO [chief executive officer] Steve Jobs put it offhandedly, the gadgets offer customers "freedom from porn"—whether they asked for it or not.

But Apple's inconsistent behavior with respect to what applications get rejected or approved, and its haphazard capitulation only when there's a public outcry, has created some mixed messages. And for a company that prides itself on quality control and a consistent product, the approach Apple is taking with app content isn't just hypocritical, it's bad for the bottom line.

Strange Adventures in Censorship

When the Wi-Fi-equipped version of the iPad went on sale two and a half months ago [April 2010], Apple demanded European magazines cover up scantily clad models for the app editions and cracked down on dictionary applications containing 'objectionable' words. They rejected a Pulitzer Prize-winning editorial cartoonist [Mark Fiore], only to rescind the rejection once the media got wind of it.

In the past week, Apple tried the same gambit with *Ulysses Seen*, a webcomic version of James Joyce's classic novel *Ulysses* featuring too much nudity for the company's taste, and an app edition of Oscar Wilde's *The Importance of Being Earnest*, which pixillated a series of panels featuring two men kissing. Both bans were reversed after considerable media outcry. (As if Joyce and Wilde haven't had to deal with enough censorship issues, already!)

Apple is, naturally, welcome to restrict the type of content that is available on its devices. And yet, as TechCrunch reported Tuesday morning [June 2010], Apple can't even keep its guidelines straight. Otherwise how would English tabloid *The Sun*'s iPad app, featuring Page Three Girls in all their topless glory, get through without incident? As InfoWorld's [executive editor for features] Galen Grunman said, "quality control over apps, such as to prevent crashes and to ensure the software does what it promises, is one thing. Control over content and thought is quite another."

It's time to think different, Apple.

Apple on Shaky Ground?

By selectively policing others, Apple demonstrates to investors and stockholders that they selectively police themselves, as well. And that puts Apple on very shaky ground.

That's because Android, Google's open-source mobile operating system, is encroaching ever-so-slowly (but steadily) on Apple's turf. While Apple's iPhone OS [operating system] (soon to be renamed iOS with the arrival of the new iPhone 4) still dominates the field with 59% of the market share, Quantcast reported that Android's share—20% as of last month [May 2010]—is growing quickly, taking 4.7% of market share from iOS over the last quarter and 8.1% of it compared with a year ago. If that trend continues, spread across devices such as the HTC EVO 4G and Motorola Droid that use Android, Apple and Google may one day find themselves in a tight race for smartphone customers. And those customers will judge whether they want a closed-when-Apple-feels-like-it iPhone or iPad app system or Android's open-for-everyone ethos.

With stiff competition gaining ground, the last thing Apple needs is to come off as indecisive. But increasingly, that's exactly how the company looks. As the dominant force in smartphones and tablets, Apple could once afford an arrogant stance, and could afford to shrug off criticism.

Now that stance appears unsustainable. The more disconnected Apple becomes from reality—and from the public that clamors for its products but grows frustrated with what they can do with them—the more impatient investors will get and the more they will demand changes. It's time to think different, Apple, and listen to the stealthy @AppleGlobalPR Twitter feed. Remember, customers are still always right. And so is common sense.

CHAPTER 3

Why Are Web-Based Mobile Apps Overtaking Native Mobile Apps?

Chapter Preface

For the past few years there has been heated debate among businesses and app developers as to whether native mobile apps are better than mobile web apps, or vice versa. Hundreds of comments about this issue appear on the Internet every month, and strong opinions are expressed. The general conclusion, however, is first, that much of the argument is meaningless since different types of apps are to be preferred in different situations; and second, that web apps may supplant native apps as technology advances.

A native mobile app is software that is produced for a specific type of device such as an iPhone or Android and runs on that device whenever it is used without being downloaded more than once. Native apps cannot run on other types of devices without being rewritten. One that works on an iPhone cannot be used on an Android phone because the devices have different operating systems. The app user must acquire a different version.

A mobile web app, on the other hand, is one in which all or some parts of the software are downloaded from the World Wide Web each time it is run. The same version can be accessed from all web-capable mobile devices through the device's web browser and in most cases is not downloaded or installed prior to use (although some newer ones can be, and will then run without being connected to the Internet). Although web apps are similar to websites, there are important differences: they are designed for the small screens of mobile devices, and unlike websites they can be launched in the same way a native device application is launched so that the user does not have to find a bookmark or remember a specific web address.

Ideally, the user of an app cannot tell the difference between a native app and a web app just by looking at what is on the screen, although there may be differences in capabilities and performance. However, the technology for creating web apps is in the process of being developed, and not all of them conform to this ideal.

Smartphones and tablets have hardware for functions that ordinary desktop computers do not have, such as making phone calls, determining a user's location, and taking pictures, Therefore the programming language that has been commonly used for creating websites is not adequate for creating web apps, and as a result, almost all mobile apps were native apps until recently. But having different programming languages for different devices leads to many problems.

Marc Hudson, a software engineer at Quicken Loans and a technology writer, discussed the history of web technology in the December 2012 issue of *Michipreneur Magazine*, explaining that until a standard programming language for creating websites was adopted the web was "a dysfunctional nightmare." Once that language was well established all websites were accessible to everyone, but then different manufacturers began producing phones that had to be programmed in other ways. "The smartphone wars had begun," he wrote. "From the onset, the . . . languages of the last decade were abandoned in the name of innovation. Unable to wait for web languages to catch up and support new hardware technologies such as GPS [Global Positioning System], touch screen gesturing, and digital cameras, the big three [mobile device manufacturers] opted to develop their native applications using vendor specific programming languages and development methodologies. Progress, once again, meant division."

If someone wants to create a native app that all mobile device owners can use, he or she must write it repeatedly in different languages for different devices. This makes it much more time-consuming and expensive than producing a web app that will work on all devices, which gives web apps a big advantage. A new programming language, HTML5, is now making it possible for the same code to be used for both websites and web apps. However, native apps written in the language of the specific mobile device on which they are run perform more efficiently than web apps, and run much faster because they can be better integrated with hardware and do not depend on Internet connection speed. So today, for most purposes native apps are still preferred; but it is expected that web languages will continue to improve.

The advantage of being able to write just one version of a web app instead of many native apps is not yet proving to be as great as many developers expected, however. HTML5 is new and so far not all its features are offered by all browsers, making it necessary to confine web apps to the capabilities common to all of them. Moreover, web apps are more difficult to distribute because they are not available in the large apps stores operated by device manufacturers, though independent app stores are starting to appear.

More and more, app developers are turning to a compromise type of app—hybrid apps. A hybrid app is written mainly in a web programming language that will work in all devices, and most of its features run on the Web; but it is surrounded by a "shell" written in the language of a specific device so that it can easily access that device's unique hardware. This means that most of it can be written just once and offered for different types of devices with relatively minor additions or modifications.

Recent Technology Has Made Development of Web-Based Mobile Apps Feasible

Ehsan

Ehsan is a senior quality assurance engineer at the Canadian technology web and mobile application development company Appnovation Technologies.

HTML5 [programming language] is a new technology that allows developers to build rich web based apps that run on any device or platform. This opens up the possibility of building the app once and running it on multiple platforms without any special translations, conversions or re-programming, using a modern, standards compliant web browser. Once a web app is launched, users on iPhones, iPads, Android phones, the Kindle Fire and Windows Phones can all access the same app and run it just as well as on any other platform. Native apps only work on the one platform they were built for, they take longer and cost more to build than a web app. This begs the question, why bother with native apps?

The answer lies with the current state of technology, which gives native apps a superior experience. This however will only last as long as we're stuck with the existing technology.

Looking at the current state of technology, we can make a comparison on what a web apps shortcomings are and in which area it is already ahead of native apps.

Distribution:

Native apps are easy to find and install. Apple store, Google Play, [Amazon's] Kindle store, [and] Microsoft app store all provide a centralized location to download any platform specific apps, with robust communities. This allows for wielding a great amount of control and influence on the distribution of the apps in the marketplace. Web apps still have quite a ways to go until a robust marketplace can be created, even ones created by independent retailers rather than operating system creators.

Advantage: Native App

Build Time and Cost:

Build time and cost is one area where web apps will shine and have clear advantage. Even though such an advantage is not apparent if the target is a single environment. Once there is a shift to multiple devices, and operating systems, the build time and cost for native apps will increase dramatically.

Advantage: Web App

Updates:

Having an out-of-date web app is virtually impossible. Think about loading a website. Each time a visitor loads a site, he or she is loading the latest version from the server. This isn't the case with native apps whose process has more of a manual component to it. Typical mobile users update their apps very infrequently; meaning the user base for a particular native app is spread across multiple versions. Web apps mean that the users will never have to worry about updates.

Advantage: Web App

Hardware Interfacing:

When it comes to interfacing with the hardware, native apps integrate seamlessly with the phone's hardware. This includes accelerometer, GPS [Global Positioning System], or camera. However, web apps are still limited to accessing only the GPS.

Advantage: Native App

Usability and Performance:

Currently, when it comes to usability and performance, native apps are unmatched in comparison to web apps. Applications tailored specifically to a certain OS [operating system] and hardware will in most cases outperform a general, web-based app.

Advantage: Native App

So, what does the future hold for web apps? There is an incredible amount of faith and energy surrounding HTML5—and a lot of that is being driven by the need to escape from the fragmentation trap that mobile has fallen into. The idea of develop it once, publish everywhere is a dream worth pursuing. The issue with performance and compatibility can be resolved fairly easily with an increase in hardware and network speeds, as well as mobile OS developers making the browsers more standards compliant. Web apps indeed have a bright and fruitful future ahead. In the next few years, with HTML5, the mobile web is destined to be the best way to share, interact with, and enjoy content on your portable device.

Mobile Cloud Apps and Hybrid Apps Take Advantage of Web Technology's Capabilities

Bill Claybrook

Bill Claybrook is president of New River Marketing Research and DirectionsonRedHat.com. He holds a doctorate in computer science.

In the past, mobile apps have been viewed as either native apps or Web apps. In this article, we include Web apps in the grouping of mobile cloud apps because they run outside the mobile device and have data storage outside the mobile device. The phrase "mobile cloud computing" typically refers to an enterprise cloud computing infrastructure [a large software package for business use] that has been extended to handle mobile devices. Users are provided with data storage and compute processing that reside on a cloud-computing platform rather than on the mobile devices themselves.

When developers build mobile apps, they have the choice of building either apps that are installed and run natively on remote devices (native apps), or those that run in mobile cloud environments (mobile cloud apps). Native apps and mobile cloud apps each have their inherent advantages and disadvantages.

Native apps run on remote devices such as smartphones and tablets and are built specifically for a device and its operating system. Native apps have the ability to leverage device-specific hardware and software, meaning that they can take advantage of the latest technology available on mobile devices, such as GPS [Global Positioning System], camera, location and locomotion. This can be construed as an advantage for native apps over mobile cloud apps.

Mobile cloud apps can be developed and made available for many devices without the need to rewrite the code.

Mobile cloud apps run on servers with their data stored in the cloud [on a server]. Users access the app through a browser window on the device. Mobile cloud apps are generally developed independent of operating systems and can be more robust than native apps because there is more compute power and storage available in the cloud than on the much smaller remote device. Mobile cloud apps present advantages over native apps because security and other management aspects can be more easily centralized.

Here are some best practices to help ensure that the mobile cloud application development process goes as smoothly and successfully as possible:

Develop Once, Run Everywhere

Because many organizations are implementing Bring your own device (BYOD) strategies, it is important to try to design and implement mobile apps that can be built once and run on multiple remote devices regardless of the device's characteristics. Mobile apps [are] developed to run natively only on the targeted devices, requiring the apps to be ported or rewritten to run on another device. Mobile cloud apps run in the cloud and are created independently of operating systems and specific device features. By using various technologies such as HTML5 [programming language] and mobile enterprise application platforms (MEAPs) [integrated group of software that provides tools for developing, deploying, and managing software running on mobile devices], mobile cloud apps can be developed and made available for many devices without the need to rewrite the code.

Hybrid apps allow mobile cloud apps to take greater advantage of mobile device hardware. With a hybrid mobile app, the user interface to the mobile cloud app appears in a browser window, with a native app wrapped around it to provide access to onboard device functionality that is not available via the browser.

A mobile platform is software that sits between a mobile device and an app.

A hybrid app looks to the user like a native app. It is downloaded from an app store, stored on the mobile device and initiated like a native app. But there is a difference from a developer point of view. The developer does not have to rewrite the entire mobile app for each device. Some of the code written in HTML5, CSS and JavaScript is reused across multiple, different mobile devices.

Use Technologies Such as HTML5 and Mobile Platforms

HTML5 is a set of technologies consisting of CSS3, rules, properties and JavaScript APIs [application programming interface]. It simplifies your development cycle by letting you use the same technology stack across multiple devices. You can deploy on more devices more quickly and easily by developing mobile cloud apps instead of native apps for a quickly growing list of mobile devices. HTML5 supports remote device functionality, providing an experience closer to the look and feel of a native app while allowing you to write code once and enable it across various mobile devices. It discovers characteristics of remote devices to present information automatically adjusted to fit the remote device's display size, resolutions, display orientation, height and other unique features.

Not all browsers, smartphones and tablets support all of the HTML5 features, but most of the major browsers support some of them. You should make sure that HTML5 is supported on the browser that you are using.

A mobile platform is software that sits between a mobile device and an app. It runs on the mobile cloud and does some tasks specifically for mobile devices, such as converting data into a user-friendly interface and making sure everything fits well on the device's screen. It also has an authentication mechanism that reaches all the way down into the device so that if it is lost or stolen, it can be wiped remotely.

MEAPs allow organizations to deploy mobile apps across a variety of devices by reusing code and without having to implement an app for a specific device. They also allow administrators to selectively run applications natively on the remote device when it is very important to take advantage of key features or when it is difficult to emulate native functionality on a mobile cloud server. . . .

Even though mobile cloud apps run on mobile cloud servers, you should synchronize application development with testing and development done for mobile devices and the technologies used to make mobile cloud apps write once and run everywhere.

The average lifespan of a mobile device is now about one year, and the lifespan of mobile software technologies is even shorter, according to technology firm Lionbridge. This challenging environment requires a new approach to software development and testing. Rather than waiting until the development of a mobile cloud app is complete, app testing needs to be in step with cloud development and device testing in order to detect and correct flaws as early in the project lifecycle as possible.

Take Advantage of Mobile Cloud Security

Running security software such as Kaspersky and McAfee and antivirus programs on mobile devices is one of the simplest ways to detect security threats. But mobile devices have limited power and processing capabilities so protecting them from threats is difficult. For instance, it is difficult, if not impossible, to keep virus detection software running continuously on a mobile device because of the device's power limitations.

Most, if not all, security threat detection capabilities can be moved from mobile devices to the mobile cloud. Multiple virtualized malware [malicious software] detection engines (running on the mobile cloud) can then be used to do the actual threat detection. This involves deploying a simple software agent on each mobile device and placing the complex, mobile device-specific detection software on the mobile cloud. The agent inspects file activity on the device, places this activity in a file, and sends the activity file to a mobile cloud service for analysis. The cloud service periodically receives activity files from agents and identifies malicious or unwanted content. A single agent activity file can be analyzed by multiple virtualized detection engines to determine if the file contains intruder attempts to compromise the mobile device.

This cloud-based approach has several benefits, including increased virus detection coverage, less complex mobile software and reduced mobile device resource consumption. This approach will become even more valuable as the scale and sophistication of mobile threats increase.

Native Mobile Apps for Publications Available on the Web Are a Short-Term Fad

Yaron Galai

Yaron Galai is the chief executive officer and the co-founder of Outbrain, a web-based recommendation engine.

A few months ago I tweeted this: "If I were a publisher I would either: a) pull my app from the App Store or b) invest *all* available cash in Apple stock." The latter piece of advice was probably pretty solid, if not very practical—Apple's stock has been performing like no other in recent history.

But my former piece of advice for publishers—to pull their apps from the App Store—doesn't seem to have resonated much, as many publishers keep pushing out their respective iPhone and iPad apps. That said, I'm betting this trend is a short-term fad that will eventually reverse, and here's why:

The Fragmented App World Is a Drain on Development Resources

The beauty of the Web is that it standardized access to information across machines, operating systems, and browsers. No more rewriting code to be Mac-, PC- and Unix-compatible, etc. Publish once on the Web, and the information will be accessible by all of humanity regardless of any configuration they might use to access it. Recently, the various app stores have again started fragmenting a world that had largely become defragmented. A fragmented dev [development] world imposes costs and headaches on those that choose to support the various apps. That might not be a huge tax on tech companies, per se, but for publishers, supporting multiple apps will become a headache and a totally unnecessary tax, which leads me to my next point.

For Most Websites, the ROI of an APP Is Unclear

A native app is a great way for developers to create functionality that's not possible with a web page (or that might otherwise require the use of Flash in a web page). Games are a perfect example of this. For a publisher whose product is words and pictures, it is unclear what additional functionality an app can provide that a well-designed Web page cannot. Sure, it's always possible to slap some artificial stuff on an app ..., but the question is whether those things are done because it's possible to do them, or because they are actually useful.

When developing a mobile app, a publisher technically becomes a node within someone else's platform—namely Apple or Google—and is bound by their rules and whims.

I'd argue that the most useful mobile reading experience is on Instapaper, which is a clean presentation of the text with proper typography—attributes that are all perfectly achievable in a well-designed mobile website. The only two exceptions here might be: a) video and b) offline reading. The gap on both is closing with HTML5, and soon even these "app excuses" won't be a valid reason for justifying development of proprietary [native] mobile apps.

You Can't Link—Or, at Least, Link Easily—to Apps

When deciding to publish content in a [native] app rather than a mobile website, it's important to understand that the value of links, as we know them on the Web, is greatly diminished. Because a [native] app is a standalone program, not a part of the open Web, linking to other pages is clunky at best. You cannot link to content on other apps. And links to websites, while possible, require switching the user to another application (AKA a mobile browser) and disrupting the user experience between articles.

You're Being Held Hostage on Someone Else's Platform

Lastly, and possibly most importantly, is the ownership of the platform on which you publish. No one owns the Web, and therefore no company can impose new rules, pricing, censorship or other surprises along the way (FCC [Federal Communications Commission] regulation aside, of course).

When developing a [native] mobile app, a publisher technically becomes a node within someone else's platform—namely Apple or Google—and is bound by their rules and whims. Apple's decision to impose a 30 percent tax on all publisher subscriptions done within apps is just one example of this. The *Financial Times* created a lot of buzz with their decision to fully withdraw from the App Store and go all-in with their mobile Web app. Developing an app for someone else's platform might give the illusion of a new marketing channel, but in reality it means becoming a node in someone else's business model.

All that said, a [native] mobile app can be a decent marketing channel, and there is value for publishers in having a presence inside the various app stores. But if you peel away all the other layers of what an app can be and focus on it exclusively as a marketing channel, then the conclusion is that *an app for publishers is basically a bookmark on people's phone screens*. That's it—a reminder to consume the publisher's content, and a quick link to do so.

I urge (and predict!) that publishers stick to these principles after the "we need to have an iPhone/iPad/Android/WebOS/Win7/etc. app" hype passes:

- Use limited dev resources to build a single, great mobile Web version of their website.

- Submit a bookmark version to all the app stores of an app that launches the Web browser with their mobile Web site.

- Use services specific to mobile, which provide readers a superior browsing experience, tailored for the mobile Web.

- Alter monetization strategies for the mobile environment, opting for revenue generators that are perfected for mobile consumption.

Mobile is putting pressure on publishers to quickly adapt and successfully deliver. In a "sink or swim" environment, the hype of apps is ultimately going to weigh publishers down. There is no real reason for publishers to spread their dev resources thin, supporting multiple proprietary [native] apps that break links and really serve someone else's strategy more than their own.

Mobile Web Apps Will Prevail Despite the Present Superiority of Native Mobile Apps

Ryan Matzner

Ryan Matzner is the chief marketing officer and lead strategist at Fueled, an iPhone and Android app development agency based in New York.

Over five years ago (on January 9th, 2007, for those of us who are counting), Steve Jobs [chief executive officer of Apple] released the original iPhone. At the time, the only apps on the iPhone were the ones that came pre-installed (think stocks, calculator and YouTube). There were so few apps, they didn't even fill up the home screen! Apple didn't provide the ability to create or install any add-on apps. Instead, developers were urged to create web apps that users would access through the built-in Safari web browser.

Facing backlash from developers, particularly in light of a community of hackers that figured out how to crack the iPhone's code and build their own apps, Apple came around and embraced native apps.

Apple's App Store contains more than 700,000 iPhone and iPad apps today. The apps available in Apple's App Store, the Google Play marketplace, and Microsoft's Windows Phone Marketplace are all "native" apps, in that developers built them using technology and code largely proprietary to those platforms. An app built for the iPhone has to be almost entirely re-coded if it's to work on a device running Google's Android operating system (a bit like translating a book from one language to another).

Then, there are web apps.

Web apps are built in standards-based technologies such as [programming languages] HTML5, CSS3 and other modern web tech. Without any special translations, conversions or re-programming, a web app can run on pretty much any platform with a modern, standards-compliant web browser. Once a web app is launched, users on iPhones, iPads, Android phones, the Kindle Fire and Windows Phones can all access the same app and run it just as well as on any other platform.

When it comes to aesthetics and overall user experience, it is incredibly difficult for web apps to trump native.

Native apps only work on the one platform they were built for, plus they take longer and cost more to build than a web app. Why then, would anyone bother building native? Current technology makes native apps a superior experience—but this is the case only for as long as we're stuck with current technology. A few advances here and there, and pretty soon native apps will go the way of desktop apps (i.e. there are still a few around but most users spend most of their time in the browser). A few elements explain why native won't rule the app roost in the future.

User Experience

Native apps tend to have a smoother look and feel, more polish. Native apps are able to leverage elements of their native operating system (i.e. rubberbanding, overscroll and slick screen transitions on iOS [Apple operating system]), so they feel more deeply integrated into the phone. When it comes to aesthetics and overall user experience, it is incredibly difficult for web apps to trump native. Furthermore, native apps come with lots of elements pre-loaded and only need to fetch user data from the web rather than the entire application, making them speedier.

The web has come a long way from the days of scrolling marquee. It's only a matter of time before the technologies behind web apps are able to compete directly with the aesthetic capabilities of native apps. Remember how marvelously advanced HTML5 seemed when it came out? Just wait 'til HTML6 or 7!

And as for having to download more data than native apps: In the future, battery life and mobile connections will be fast enough that it won't matter. 4G download speeds are actually faster than the average U.S. broadband connection, and when was the last time you worried about the size of a website loading on your desktop?

Distribution

Native apps are easy to find and install. The Apple App Store, Google Play, etc. are great places to browse for and download apps. The hard part of building a successful app store is creating a robust developer community willing to devote the time, effort and money to build lots of great apps that users want to use. That's a tall order, and is probably the biggest part of why Microsoft is struggling to gain traction with Windows Phone.

One caveat to this whole web app thing is competition. Apple, Google and even Microsoft must be particularly content with the great control and influence they wield by controlling distribution for their platforms via app stores and marketplaces. As web apps pick up steam and begin to threaten mobile apps, it's likely that current stakeholders will push back against anything that devalues their native app stores. Fortunately for consumers, there's probably not a whole lot anyone can do to stop the impending march of web apps. Robust web browsers being baked into the OS [operating system] aren't going anywhere.

With web apps, there's no need to convince developers to create software for a specific platform. Instead, apps created for users on the most popular platforms will also work for users on the least popular platforms, assuming that platform has a decent web browser. In the future, app stores can be created by independent retailers rather than operating system creators. Directory sites such as Best Vendor and Listio might grow to rival Apple's App Store.

Web apps mean that users will never have to worry about updates.

Build Time and Cost

A typical native app takes a bit longer to build than an equivalent web app would, but as developer tools and education improve, that will likely change. And as more developers become versed in the development languages and technologies used to create native apps, overall app development costs will fall.

But one thing that likely won't change in the world of native apps is that building for multiple platforms and devices is expensive. Adding iPad compatibility when building an iPhone app can add up to 50% to the development costs of a project. When rumors began swirling that Apple might release an iPad Mini, we wondered, *who has the budget to build for all these screen sizes?*

Web apps will work on devices across a range of sizes by being adaptive and responsive.

[Updates are] an area where web apps already trump native. Much to the chagrin of developers, typical mobile users update their apps very infrequently. That means the user base for a particular native app is spread across multiple versions. A friend recently exclaimed his surprise that Instagram wasn't working properly on his iPhone. It turns out he hadn't updated the app in a while and was using an unsupported old version.

Having an out-of-date web app is virtually impossible. Think about loading a website. Each time a visitor loads a site, he or she is loading the latest version off the server. When Google updates the logo on their homepage, seeing it doesn't require users to go and download an update to Google—the mere action of visiting the site means the user is viewing the latest version.

Web apps mean that users will never have to worry about updates.

Hardware Interfacing

One of the things that make native apps so delightful to use is their ability to leverage the phone's hardware so seamlessly. Think about all the great apps that use your phone's accelerometer (Nike+), GPS [Global Positioning System] (Foursquare) or camera (Instagram). Of those three, web apps can only access GPS and even then, only in a limited capacity. Yes, that's right—web apps can't even use your phone's camera or access photos you've already taken.

There's no standard way for web apps to access hardware on mobile devices, but that's relatively easy to change in future updates. One issue to overcome is potential security concerns, but probably the biggest hurdle is a lack of cooperation from entrenched interests that would prefer to keep a native app monopoly in place. Nonetheless, competitive pressures in the app and phone OS space will eventually force devices to become more open.

Credit Cards

Apple users are notoriously voracious consumers. Apple's secret weapon is that it has 400 million active iTunes accounts with credit cards on file. And having a credit card on file makes app purchases a breeze—tap "buy" and enter a password—that's it! Google and Microsoft surely have far fewer active accounts on their platforms, but those numbers are growing. The bottom line is that purchasing native apps and making in-app purchases is exceedingly easy.

There is no consolidated payment system for purchasing web apps or buying web app add-ons, but that will change over time as players like PayPal, Square, Venmo and others jump into the space.

A huge part of the success of iOS is attributed to Apple's App Store, much as the iTunes music store is a big part of why the iPod was such a hit. And yet, the App Store's undoing will likely be the web apps that Apple originally promoted in lieu of native apps.

CHAPTER 4

What Effect Is the App Economy Having on Society?

Chapter Preface

As of 2013, the boom in production and use of mobile apps, often referred to as the "App Economy," is creating great excitement in the business world. It is estimated that it has created about half a million jobs, including those related to the production and sale of apps as well as the creation of them by programmers. This is an important trend in an era in which employment in many other fields is falling. It has led to a new and unexpected change in the way software is developed and marketed.

Until recently, from the user's standpoint the Internet was almost synonymous with the World Wide Web. Apart from e-mail, contact with the Internet meant accessing it through a web browser on a desktop or laptop computer. But now, it is estimated that nearly two-thirds of people connect to the web via a smartphone, tablet, or on-the-go laptop, and by many of them, mobile apps are used more than websites. In fact, the use of apps has become so prevalent that some experts believe they will replace websites almost entirely. According to a 2012 report by the Pew Research Center on the future of the Internet, "This is not just a debate about technology use and which businesses will prevail. It involves different visions of the way that people will access information, learn, amuse themselves, and create material with others in the digital era."

A controversial article in the September 2010 issue of *Wired* by Chris Anderson and Michael Wolff proclaimed that "The Web is Dead, Long Live the Internet." In Anderson and Wolff's opinion, people are choosing apps over websites because they "often just work better or fit better into their lives (the screen comes to them, they don't have to go to the screen). The fact that it's easier for companies to make money on these platforms only cements the trend."

However, by no means has everyone agreed that Web use is declining. In response to the *Wired* article's graph of the alleged decline, the *New York Times* wrote, "The graph . . . doesn't say that we're using the Web less. It just says that we're using a lot more online tools. Actually, what it really says is that online video has taken off in the last few years (well, duh), which totally skews the 'percentage of Internet traffic' statistic. . . . A more responsible, accurate article would have been titled, 'The Web Remains Increasingly Popular, Even as It Is Joined by More and More Special-Purpose Internet Apps.'"

Some commentators, while disagreeing that the Web is "dead," nevertheless believe that mobile apps will become overwhelmingly dominant. In April 2011, *Time* magazine stated, "To be clear, the Web will never die, it'll just go the way of snail mail or vinyl records." But this view, like many other enthusiastic comments about the rise of mobile apps, overlooks some important questions, such what specific types of Internet uses are being considered, and what users the writer is thinking about.

The people who write about economics, or about technical issues related to the Internet and software development, tend to be relatively affluent individuals who use the most advanced technology in their work and in their daily lives. They observe what they and others in similar positions are doing. What is often forgotten is that not everybody can afford a smartphone or tablet. The number of people who do have smartphones is large and growing, but it will be a long time before everyone with access to the Internet has one. Moreover, discussions of the relative merits of apps vs. websites are often centered on value to businesses and advertisers. Yet many people who use websites are not in the market for the products advertised online; they use them only for social networking and information. Often they need more detailed information than can be shown on a small screen.

Therefore, the common assertion that "everybody" is abandoning websites for apps cannot be taken too literally. Nevertheless, the popularity of mobile apps has transformed the software industry, and it is safe to say that the demand for them will continue to grow.

It's Not Just Instagram. The "App Economy" Is Taking Off

Meredith Bennett-Smith

Meredith Bennett-Smith is the cover story intern for the Christian Science Monitor, *where she assists with weekly feature packages as well the day-to-day functions of its parenting blog.*

Three years ago, frustrated in his search for a summer job, Valparaiso University senior Cameron Banga decided to try less traditional work: writing apps.

It was a crazy idea. Apple's iPhone was only two years old, and its app store—where Mr. Banga hoped to sell his programs—had opened just the previous summer. Nevertheless, with two college buddies and more confidence than experience, Banga watched a brief computer science class posted online and got down to writing what he hoped would be one really good piece of software.

The result? A battery-monitoring application for the iPhone called Battery Go! Within 36 hours of its release, the free software had rocketed to No. 70 on the Top 100 iPhone apps list. "It was this kind of modern-day gold rush," Banga recalls. "We were really fortunate. We had the right idea at the right time."

Banga and his two partners are members of the new "app economy," a burgeoning industry of mini-software at micro prices. Nevertheless, the sector has spawned nearly $20 billion in sales and 466,000 jobs, according to one recent study, and it shows no signs of slowing down. In a national economy stuck in low gear, the app economy is providing some pop to America's jobs engine that could, in a few years, make a measurable difference.

"Whenever you create a new medium of communication, a new consumer medium of communication, you inevitably have revolutionary changes," says Paul Saffo, managing director at Discern, an investment analytics firm based in San Francisco. "Anything this size is, of course, going to have a multiplier effect across industries."

Apps are a diverse group of low-cost, lightweight software programs, often designed for portable devices, that users can download with the touch of a button, often for 99 cents or even free of charge. (Many firms rely on ads for revenue.) While the names of leading app companies might not be familiar, the games, online tools, and productivity software they've created are known by anyone who owns a smart phone or a tablet computer, or uses social media. From FarmVille (Zynga) to Angry Birds (Rovio) to Mint.com (Quicken) to the camera application Instagram, there seems to be an app to meet just about any need or desire. There are nearly 1 million of them for iPhone, iPad, and Android devices alone.

Unlike building smart phones or creating PC software, apps are small and quicker to develop.

In a recent indication of the growing status—and market value—of applications, Facebook said this week it is shelling out $1 billion to acquire the hip photo-sharing smartphone app, Instagram. With its 30 million iPhone users [of devices using the Apple operating system], and even more projected to sign up because of its recent expansion to the Android [operating system] platform, Facebook's newest investment could mean 100 million more global users in the next year.

"Really, what you're talking about is a massive transformation in the way that people live their lives," says Michael Mandel, chief economic strategist for the Progressive Policy Institute, a Washington think tank, and author of the study that counted nearly 500,000 jobs related to the app economy. "I wouldn't call this a small-company phenomenon. . . . Small companies are important, but what you've seen is small companies that turn into big companies."

The app revolution is happening more quickly and on a broader scale than the personal-computer revolution of the 1980s.

Large companies anchor the industry by offering platforms for which the apps are written: Android is anchored by Google, Apple iOS by Apple, and Windows Phone and Windows Mobile by Microsoft. Facebook has encouraged the development of many Facebook apps.

One characteristic of the app economy is that, for startups at least, the barrier to entry is low. This is an advantage. Unlike building smart phones or creating PC [personal computer] software, apps are small and quicker to develop.

"In the past, with computer software, it would be almost impossible to create something in a month, sell it, and make any money," Banga says. The ease of one-touch buying and the low costs of most applications make it easy for consumers to buy apps over the life of the machine and on a whim, says Mr. Saffo.

The result: The app revolution is happening more quickly and on a broader scale than the personal-computer revolution of the 1980s.

But a low barrier to entry also means that start-ups can disappear quickly, even after initial success. One example is Banga's initial firm, CollegeKidApp.com. After graduation, the firm's founders parted ways. Banga created a new app-design and development company, 9magnets LLC, with new partners.

In its first full business year, 9magnets brought in six figures in revenue and is covering its expenses. That financial stability is unusual.

"Most of the app developers springing up will crash and burn—that's typical of start-ups, especially in tech," says David Truog, vice president and research director in interactive marketing at Forrester Research, a global research and advisory firm based in Cambridge, Mass. But "it's a shift that's resulting in a whole new market and is creating a lot of wide-open opportunity."

For now, the established platform companies face better prospects. Facebook has been an especially savvy innovator in making money from social media. According to Inside Network, the social networking giant made $4 billion in revenue last year [2011] and $1 billion in profit.

"We estimate in the US the virtual good market [on Facebook] will bring in $2.1 billion this year," says Justin Smith, founder of Inside Network, a San Francisco-based news and market research firm.

Saffo estimates that the app boom will take five to 10 years to mature.

"The whole notion of an app is going to evolve dramatically and rapidly . . . and devices are going to evolve rapidly as well," he says. "We'll look back and laugh and nudge each other, 'Remember when we bought Angry Birds?' But this is a permanent change on the landscape; it's no fad. Anybody who underestimates the scale of the app revolution is greatly mistaken."

The App Economy Will Improve the US Employment Rate if Open Jobs Can Be Filled

Amrita Khalid

Amrita Khalid is a Future Tense project intern at the online magazine Slate.

"This is shameless, really," said Rep. Mary Bono Mack, R-Calif., on Wednesday [September 2012], as she held out her iPad, showing a high-resolution photo of her infant grandson to those gathered in the Rayburn [congressional office building] hearing room.

But this wasn't just a grandmother showing off. Recently, the chairwoman of the House Subcommittee for Commerce, Manufacturing, and Trade said, she had been babysitting her grandson when he was struck in the middle of the night with "a crying fit. . . . So I did anything any good grandmother would do, and I went to the [Apple] App Store and downloaded Baby Soother"—the app version of the Baby Einstein[-branded] product created by New York-based app developer IntuApps.

The eight-term congresswoman was trying to make the point that the average American has become so app-enabled that if we come across a problem, we expect to find an app solution. That's an exaggeration—more than half of American adults don't own a smartphone.

Nevertheless, in just five years, mobile apps have become a $20 billion industry. The Apple Store has grown from 500 apps in 2008, the year it launched, to more than 600,000. One industry group reports that there were 11 billion downloads of apps in 2010 and anticipates that figure will grow to 77 billion by 2014—that's more than 10 apps downloaded for every person alive on the planet today. The booming mobile app market has created roughly 466,000 jobs since 2007, according to a study released in February [2012] by TechNet. And the app industry says that there could be more—if Congress cooperates.

That's why, under the pressure of a dismal September jobs report and upcoming election, this hearing on the future of the "app economy" took place in the first week Congress was back in session.

The four-member panel that testified before the subcommittee included representatives from small-business app-developers FastCustomer and Flurry Inc., plus the tech industry trade associations TechNet and the Association for Competitive Technology. The figures they boasted were the stuff of political dreams: The apps industry is American born and bred. Seventy-eight percent of app companies are small businesses. Many are women-owned. U.S. app developers even command a 22 percent of Chinese app market revenues.

Yet several potential snags loom.

In just five years, mobile apps have become a $20 billion industry.

App Developers Need More Spectrum

As developers continue innovating, their faster, stronger, and more productive apps will eat up bandwidth like it's no joke. The faster 4G networks are creating a spectrum shortage, and industry heads are asking lawmakers to free up spectrum, most of which is government-owned. So in February [2012] Congress passed legislation allowing the FCC [Federal Communications Commission] to hold spectrum auctions to free up both licensed and unlicensed spectrum for wireless broadband. The agency will meet on Sept. 28 to figure out exactly how to do this.

App Developers Need More People

An estimated 44,000 open developer jobs will have no impact on the unemployment rate if they go unfilled. In a survey conducted by app developer Flurry, more than three-fourths of respondents said they don't think their companies can hire all of the software developers they need. And they're not exactly looking to give positions to laid-off auto workers in Michigan. When asked during the hearing how his company recruits its employees, Peter Farago, VP of Flurry Inc., looked uncomfortable when he replied they usually hired the cream of crop from the Ivy League [colleges] and top technical schools such as MIT [Massachusetts Institute of Technology] and CalTech [California Institute of Technology].

Private mobile-app developers are looking to Congress to help address this human capital shortage, which Rey Ramsey, the CEO [chief executive officer] of TechNet, blames on "a string of policy problems tracing back to schools." With the federal government struggling to staff its own technology workforce, this might be a tall order.

App Developers May Face More Scrutiny in How They Handle Data

After Bono Mack flashed her grandson's photo for the world to see, Rep. Bill Cassidy, R-La., bought up the point of ownership. Does Bono Mack really own Baby Sonny's photo? Or does the app company that she used to store it? And what prevented the company from stealing the photo and using it in something like a Gerber commercial?

While Cassidy's example was a little far-fetched (not to mention already illegal), the sentiment was spot-on. That very morning, Rep. Ed Markey, D-Mass., introduced the Mobile

Device Privacy Act, which would require mobile companies or app developers to let consumers know in advance if their personal activity is being tracked, why it's being tracked, and who is seeing it.

Until now, the app industry has enjoyed relatively little regulation, allowing it to flourish—but also creating some disasters. Welcome to the Age of Transparency, App Economy.

Independent App Developers Earn Far Less Money than Salaried Ones

Joshua Wright

Joshua Wright is a member of the marketing team at Economic Modeling Specialists International.

The *New York Times* [*NYT*] continued [in 2012] its excellent iEconomy series with an article on the job prospects for app developers. The lengthy piece gives a few snippets of labor market data for software developers and touches on the work of economist Michael Mandel in measuring the "App Economy."

The gist of the *NYT* piece, and something that Mandel doesn't go along with, is that the majority of entrepreneurs in the app writing realm have a difficult time making a living—despite all the buzz that surrounds the growing field.

Mandel's recent paper on the subject "makes it clear that large companies are hiring droves of app developers in-house to create and maintain apps," he writes on his blog. (Note: Mandel's paper was written for a software development industry association, and his previous App Economy paper was written for advocacy group TechNet.)

Using all this as a jumping-off point, we explored EMSI's [Economic Modeling Specialists International] data on software developers—both those in traditional employment settings and those who are self-employed or write code on the side. Our analysis shows that while wages for independent app developers significantly lag those of salaried employees in the field, proprietors have grown at a faster pace than their salaried counterparts in app development over the last decade.

Mandel relied on job posting data for his research. For this post, we used standard labor market data from EMSI—understanding its limitations in measuring relatively new occupations such as this one—and specifically focused on application software developers. Not all these workers create mobile apps for the iPhone or Android mobile operating system, but this is the closest we can get to approximating the labor market characteristics of app developers with historic, detail-rich data.

Fast Job Growth

Mandel estimates there are 519,000 jobs in the App Economy, with only a portion of those being app developers. Meanwhile, as the *Times* writes, there are roughly one million software developer jobs in the U.S., and the growth has been robust outside hiccups during the 2001 and 2007–2009 recessions. When we narrow our focus to application software developers, removing systems software developers from the picture, the national job total shrinks to fewer than 570,000. Self-employed app developers and those who work on the side on top of their primary job (what EMSI refers to as "extended proprietors") account for another 40,000-plus estimated jobs, or 7% of the total app developer workforce as of 2012.

We should note here that EMSI's proprietor datasets offer a window into entrepreneurial activity for app developers and any other occupation, but we caution against labeling *all* workers in the self-employed or extended proprietor classes as entrepreneurs. More accurately, inside the extended proprietors dataset are those who pursue extra work opportunities while maintaining their day job, while the self-employed dataset includes those who have taken the additional step and are primarily on their own. Once start-up owners incorporate their business, they fall under the traditional wage-and-salary worker datasets.

The U.S. has nearly twice as many proprietors classified as generic computer programmers as app developers—and nearly three times as many proprietors [who are] information security analysts, web developers, and computer network architects. Still, with proprietors and salaried employees taken together, there are more app developers than any programming-related occupation, and it's the second-highest paying programming-related occupation behind systems software developers.

[Note] that 7% of application software developers nationwide are either self-employed or write code as a side gig.

Lower Earnings for Independent Workers

What's really eye-opening, however, is the difference in hourly earnings for salaried app developers and independent app developers. The wages for proprietors are substantially lower than their traditional counterparts. The earnings disparity for app developers at the bottom 10% in wages—what can be considered entry level—isn't huge, but it quickly escalates. At the median wage level, salaried app developers make 1.5 times more than proprietors ($43.18 vs. $28.22 per hour); that jumps to almost twice as much among the top 10% of earners ($63.45 vs. $32.13).

This wage gap isn't confined to app developers; across the board, self-employed workers and extended proprietors make far less. But what stands out for application developers is how dramatically the gap widens for salaried workers from the bottom to top 10th percentile of workers, and how comparatively small that gap is for proprietors. The top earners among proprietors make just $8 more per hour more than the bottom 10th percentile; for salaried workers, the difference is $36 per hour (or an additional $75,000 per year).

We've already mentioned that 7% of application software developers nationwide are either self-employed or write code as a side gig. That's up from 6.8% in 2001. Not a huge bump. But this segment of the app developer workforce has grown 13% since 2001, compared to 9% growth for standard salaried workers. Since 2007, when the App Economy took off, each group of workers has grown 6%.

Developers Use Many Tactics to Increase the Earning Power of Their Apps

Priya Viswanathan

Priya Viswanathan is a contributing writer for several websites and blogs relating to electronic gear and mobile devices and applications.

With so many types of mobile devices and new mobile OS' [operating systems] coming into the market today, app development is emerging more profitable than ever before. The app developer, even about 5 years ago, had a limited choice of mobile OS' such as Windows Mobile, BlackBerry and Apple. But today, with the emergence of so many new mobile platforms and their different versions; also with the concept of cross-platform formatting of apps getting more popular; the field of mobile app development becomes a veritable treasure-trove for the developer to make a decent sum of money every month, by way of creating mobile applications.

In this article, we discuss ways and means you can use to make the maximum money from mobile app development.

Highly Profitable Business

All the major app stores such as the Apple App Store, the Google Android Market, RIM's App World, the Nokia Ovi Store and so on, have already made billions of dollars in terms of profit, over the last few years. Mobile apps have now emerged as one of the easiest and best ways to advertise and sell products and services, encourage social sharing of information and generally encourage mobile users towards developing and maintaining brand loyalty.

The mobile app development market is vast and offers great scope for app developers and companies to succeed beyond their expectation, by making very little initial investment. Angry Birds is one great game app that has maintained its immense popularity among the masses. While many other such apps have been successful, this one has emerged a top-selling app, by making the maximum amount of revenue for its creator, Rovio.

Very few [apps] . . . are capable of generating the kind of revenue that the biggest players did.

The Secret Formula of Mobile App Success

There are several thousands of popular apps out there, which have been downloaded millions of times by users. But very few among them are capable of generating the kind of revenue that the biggest players did. The actual reason behind this has nothing to do with the company's lack of insight.

Quoting the example of Angry Birds once again, Rovio had released a free version of the app for the Android Market. This version also came with an advertising bar on it and this is exactly where the actual revenue came from. Today, the company still manages to earn much more from these adverts rather than from the actual sales of the app.

Of course, the success of an app depends upon the number of people using it, and also amount of time they spend on it. Rovio is an established company that has had years of app development experience behind it. The developer team focused on trying to engage mobile users, creating a game that would encourage them to repeatedly use the app. The company came out with regular app updates, also releasing free versions of the updates, which were eagerly lapped up by its audience. Angry Birds is now much more than a mere mobile app—it is now a brand name, which boasts of users from all over the world.

Using Mobile Social Sharing to Advantage

Developing mobile social apps is a great way of achieving success in the app marketplace. This encourages users to share the information with their friends online, with very little extra effort on the part of the app developer. Mobile services such as Facebook and Twitter are the finest examples of such apps, which are a rage among the current generation of users.

While developing social apps may not rake in massive returns, combining this with in-app purchasing would be a great way for developers to attract much more revenue from their app. As far as mobile social gaming is concerned, the developer could possibly offer users a completely ad-free version of the game at a nominal fee. Certain games also make money by encouraging users to purchase virtual cash or enhanced game themes for small sums of money. This technique, while effective, also takes a lot of time and effort on the part of the app developer.

Partnering with Mobile Brands and Carriers

Several app developers and companies are now partnering with mobile brands and carriers to release their apps with them. This could become a win-win situation if it works as intended. However, the app developer would enjoy only a fraction of the revenue in this case, as he or she would have to pass on a large percentage of the profits to the mobile device brand or carrier concerned.

Besides, each of these brands or carriers may have their own stipulation regarding the look and feel of the app. This could end up curbing the developer's creativity. Nevertheless, this is a good opportunity for new app developers to showcase their work and get noticed in the app marketplace.

The App Economy Has Transformed the Strategy of Software Development

Mark Mulligan

Mark Mulligan is a British musician and music industry analyst who writes a well-known blog. He is frequently quoted and interviewed by top TV, radio, print, and online media.

Mobile apps can stake a pretty solid claim to being the single most important shift in consumer product behaviour in the last 5 years. Sure the devices themselves are pivotally important, but were it not for the apps consumers install on them, they would just be better versions of the feature phones and early smartphones from half a decade earlier. Apps have transformed consumers' expectations of what digital experiences should be, and not just on connected devices. But Apps have also transformed product strategy, in two key ways:

- Apps have replaced product strategy with feature strategy
- Apps have created a renaissance in the consumer software market

Apps Have Replaced Product Strategy with Feature Strategy

Though there are a good number of apps which can be genuinely held up as fully fledged products (Google Maps, Angry Birds, WhatsApp etc.) many are in fact product features rather than products. Shazam for example is a fantastic feature, so fantastic that it should be as ubiquitous in music products as a volume button, but it is nonetheless a feature not a product. Don't mistake this for a derogatory critique: indeed feature strategy is virtually the core DNA [basis of development] of the app model. After all, apps rely upon the core product of the smartphone or tablet itself to do much of the hard work.

Apps co-exist with the core functionality of the device in order to layer extra features on top. Instagram uses a phone's camera and web functionality, Layar uses the camera and GPS [Global Positioning System] and so forth. In short, apps add features and functionality to hardware products. That does not make them inherently any less valuable for doing so, but it does make them dramatically different from pre-App products. Even the majority of utility apps, such as those that track rail and flight schedules, or the weather are at heart browser bookmarks on steroids. Games are perhaps the only app category which in the main can be considered as self-contained products.

Apps have enabled the consumer software market to finally reach its true opportunity.

This shift from product strategy to feature strategy has slashed the time it takes for products to get to market and has dramatically reduced development overhead, but it is a model riven with risk. Consumers and the device ecosystem companies are winners, but many app developers are exposed. On the one hand they have the insecurity associated with platform dependency, on the other they know that if their features are *that* good that they will likely be integrated into the device's core OS [operating system] or into the featureset of another app with broader functionality. Sometimes those scenarios will be achieved via favourable commercial avenues (such as an acquisition or licensing) but sometimes it will just be flat out plagiarism.

The lesson for app developers is clear: if your app is a feature and it is good, then you need to plan for how to turn it into a product, or else plan for what to do when your app has become someone else's feature.

Apps Have Created a Renaissance in the Consumer Software Market

It is sometimes easy to lose sight of just what apps are: software. In the PC [personal computer] age software was for most people one of three things:

- Microsoft Windows and Office

- An anti-virus tool

- A bunch of free-trial *bloatware* shortcuts preinstalled on their desktop pre point of sale

Mainstream PC behaviour was defined by Microsoft functionality and browser based activity. Sure, software from the likes of Real Networks and Adobe supported much of those browser based experiences, but they were to the consumer effectively extensions of the core OS rather than software products themselves. A premium consumer software market did exist but never broke through to mainstream. Consumers didn't know where to look for software, whether it would install properly, whether it would work on their PC, and then on top of all this they were faced with having to provide credit card details to small companies they knew nothing about.

Mobile apps changed all of that. App stores simultaneously fixed the discovery, billing, installation and compatibility issues in one fair swoop. Apps have enabled the consumer software market to finally reach its true opportunity. Just in the same way that the iPod allowed digital music to fulfil its potential.

So where will feature strategy and the reinvigorated consumer software business take us? What is clear is that consumers are getting exposed to a wider array of digital experiences and are evolving more sophisticated digital behaviours due to apps. Apps are also enabling consumers to do things more effectively and efficiently, and are empowering them with more information to make better decisions, whether that be getting the best flight price or choosing the best local plumber. They are also making consumers expect a lot more from a device's ecosystem than just the devices. How often do you see a phone company advertise its handsets with the screen turned off? It is the apps that count. For now, however good Nokia might be able to make its smartphones it knows that its app catalogue and ecosystem struggles to hold a candle to Apple's App store and ecosystem (the same of course applies to all other handset manufacturers).

Apps Have Become Velvet Handcuffs for Connected Device Owners

But what happens if/when consumers start to shift at scale between ecosystems? For example, say Apple finds swathes of its iPhone and iPad customers switching to competitors in the future, what sort of backlash will occur when consumers find they have to expensively reassemble their app collections to reconstruct the features they grew used to on their Apple devices? Perhaps a smart handset manufacturer would consider investing in an *app amnesty*, giving new customers the equivalents of their iOS [Apple Operating System] apps for free on their new handsets.

For now though, Apple's market leading app catalogue behaves like velvet handcuffs on its customers and gives it a *product strategy grace period*, in which it could get away with having a sub-par product generation, with customers staying loyal because of not wanting to lose their app collections. But not even the strength of Apple's app catalogue would not enable them to keep hold of disaffected customers much longer than that. After all, apps are features, not the product itself.

Organizations to Contact

The editors have compiled the following list of organizations concerned with the issues debated in this book. The descriptions are derived from materials provided by the organizations. All have publications or information available for interested readers. The list was compiled on the date of publication of the present volume; names, addresses, phone and fax numbers, and e-mail and Internet addresses may change. Be aware that many organizations take several weeks or longer to respond to inquiries, so allow as much time as possible.

Center for Democracy and Technology (CDT)
1634 I St. NW, #1100, Washington, DC   20006
(202) 637-9800 • fax: (202) 637-0968
website: www.cdt.org

CDT's mission is to develop public policy solutions that advance constitutional civil liberties and democratic values in new computer and communications media. Pursuing its mission through policy research, public education, and coalition building, the center works to increase citizens' privacy and the public's control over the use of personal information held by government and other institutions. Its publications include issue briefs, policy papers, and CDT Policy Posts.

CTIA—The Wireless Association
1400 16th St. NW, Suite 600, Washington, DC   20036
(202) 736-3200 • fax: (202) 785-0721
website: www.ctia.org

CTIA is an international nonprofit membership organization that has represented the wireless communications industry since 1984. The association advocates on behalf of its members at all levels of government. CTIA also coordinates the industry's voluntary efforts to provide consumers with a variety of choices and information regarding their wireless products and services. This includes the voluntary industry guidelines, programs that promote mobile device recycling and reusing, and wireless accessibility for individuals with disabilities. Online, the association offers a blog, e-mail news briefings, and multimedia library.

Electronic Frontier Foundation (EFF)
815 Eddy St., San Francisco, CA 94109
(415) 436-9333 • fax: (415) 436-9993
e-mail: info@eff.org
website: www.eff.org

EFF is an organization of students and other individuals that aims to promote a better understanding of telecommunications issues. It fosters awareness of civil liberties issues arising from advancements in computer-based communications media and supports litigation to preserve, protect, and extend First Amendment rights in computing and telecommunications technologies. EFF's publications include the electronic newsletter *EFFector Online*, online bulletins, and publications, including *Know Your Digital Rights' Guide: Guard Against 4th Amendment Violations*.

Electronic Privacy Information Center (EPIC)
1718 Connecticut Ave. NW, Suite 200, Washington, DC 20009
(202) 483-1140 • fax: (202) 483-1248
website: www.epic.org

As an advocate of the public's right to electronic privacy, EPIC sponsors educational and research programs, compiles statistics, and conducts litigation pertaining to privacy and other civil liberties. Its publications include the biweekly electronic newsletter *EPIC Alert* and reports such as "Smartphones and Election 2012."

Federal Trade Commission (FTC)
600 Pennsylvania Ave. NW, Washington, DC 20580
(202) 326-2222
website: www.ftc.gov

The FTC deals with issues that touch the economic life of every American. It is the only federal agency with both consumer protection and competition jurisdiction in broad sectors of the economy. Its website offers information on mobile telecommunications, handheld devices, and smartphone applications, including issues relating to consumer privacy.

Mobile Marketing Association (MMA)

PO Box 3963, Bellevue, WA   98009-3963
(646) 257-4515
e-mail: mma@mmaglobal.com
website: www.mmaglobal.com

MMA is a nonprofit trade association representing all players in the mobile marketing value chain. It works to promote, educate, measure, guide, and protect the mobile marketing industry worldwide. One of the association's objectives is to define and publish mobile marketing best practices and guidelines on privacy, ad delivery, and ad measurement. The association publishes a newsletter and the *International Journal of Mobile Marketing*.

Privacy International

46 Bedford Row, London   WC1R 4LR
   UK
+44 (0) 20 7242 2836
e-mail: info@privacy.org
website: www.privacyinternational.org

Privacy International is a nongovernmental organization with members in forty countries around the world. Its primary goal is to promote an international understanding of the importance of protecting individual privacy and personal data. Privacy International's website provides reports, studies, and commentary on current policy and technology issues, and also includes an online archive of information for students and researchers.

Privacy Rights Clearinghouse (PRC)
3108 Fifth Ave., Suite A, San Diego, CA   92103
(619) 298-3396
website: www.privacyrights.org

PRC is a nonprofit consumer organization with a two-part mission—to provide consumer information and advocate for consumer privacy. The group raises awareness of how technology affects personal privacy, empowers consumers to take action to control their own personal information by providing practical tips on privacy protection, responds to privacy-related complaints from consumers, and reports this information. Its website provides transcripts of PRC speeches and testimony, stories of consumer experiences, and numerous fact sheets, including "Hang Up on Harassment: Dealing with Cellular Phone Abuse" and "Privacy in the Age of the Smartphone."

Bibliography

Books

Daniel A. Begun   *Amazing Android Apps for Dummies.*
Hoboken, NJ: Wiley, 2011.

Barry Burd   *Android Application Development
All-in-One for Dummies.* Hoboken,
NJ: Wiley, 2011.

Harry J. Dickens   *Apps for Learning: 40 Best
and Andrew   iPad/iPhone Apps for High School
Churches   Classrooms.* Vancouver, British
Columbia: Corwin, 2012.

Lyza Danger   *Head First Mobile Web.* Sebastopol,
Gardner and   CA: O'Reilly, 2011.
Jason Grigsby

Jinny   *iPad Apps for Kids for Dummies.*
Gudmundsen   Hoboken, NJ: Wiley, 2012.

Wallace Jackson   *Android Apps for Absolute Beginners.*
New York: Apress, 2012.

Bob LeVitus and   *Incredible iPad Apps for Dummies.*
Bryan Chaffin   Hoboken, NJ: Wiley, 2010.

Rory Lewis and   *iPhone and iPad Apps for Absolute
Chad Mello   Beginners.* New York: Apress, 2013.

Dan Marcolina   *iPhone Obsessed: Photo Editing
Experiments with Apps.* Berkeley, CA:
Peachpit Press, 2011.

Chad Mureta   *App Empire: Make Money, Have a
Life, and Let Technology Work for You.*
Hoboken, NJ: Wiley, 2012.

Jakob Nielsen and *Mobile Usability*. Berkeley, CA: New
Raluca Budiu   Riders, 2012.

Peggy Anne Salz   *The Everything Guide to Mobile Apps:*
and Jennifer   *A Practical Guide to Affordable Mobile*
Moranz   *App Development for Your Business.*
                   Avon, MA: Adams Media, 2013.

Michael Saylor   *The Mobile Wave: How Mobile*
                   Intelligence Will Change Everything.
                   Philadelphia, PA: Vanguard, 2012.

Janine Warner   *Mobile Web Design for Dummies.*
and David   Hoboken, NJ: Wiley, 2010.
LaFontaine

Jeremy Warner   *Best Mobile Apps: Top Developers*
                   Share Their Secrets to Success. Vernon
                   Hills, IL: Portrait Health, 2013.
                   (ebook only)

Carla White   *Idea to iPhone: The Essential Guide to*
                   Creating Your First App for the iPhone
                   and iPad. Hoboken, NJ: Wiley, 2013.

Ken Yarmosh   *App Savvy: Turning Ideas into iPad*
                   and iPhone Apps Customers Really
                   Want. Sebastopol, CA: O'Reilly, 2011.

Periodicals and Internet Resources

David Alexander   "Pentagon Unveils Plan to Tap
                   Potential of Mobile Devices," Reuters,
                   February 26, 2013. www.reuters.com.

Janna Anderson   "The Future of Apps and Web," Pew
and Lee Rainie   Internet, March 23, 2012.
                   http://pewinternet.org.

Scott Austin and
Andrew Dowell

"'Girls Around Me' Developer Defends App After Foursquare Dismissal," *Wall Street Journal* blog, March 31, 2012. http://blogs.wsj.com.

Tim Berners-Lee

"Long Live the Web: A Call for Continued Open Standards and Neutrality," *Scientific American*, November 22, 2010. www.scientificamerican.com.

Ciaran Bradley

"The Rise of the Rogue App and How to Protect Against Them," *Huffington Post*, May 10, 2012. www.huffingtonpost.co.uk.

Daniel Donahoo

"The Future of Apps for Young Children: Beyond ABC & 123," *Huffington Post*, August 13, 2012. www.huffingtonpost.com.

Andrew Dowell

"Tracking Women: Now There's Not an App for That," *Wall Street Journal* blog, March 31, 2012. http://blogs.wsj.com.

Prue Duggan

"Smartphones and the Evolution of the App," *Backbase*, January 31, 2013. http://blog.backbase.com.

Rose Eveleth

"In an Era of Mobile Apps, Is There Room for the Children's Toy?" SmartPlanet, December 13, 2012. www.smartplanet.com.

Federal Trade Commission "Mobile Apps for Kids: Current Privacy Disclosures Are Disappointing," February 2012. http://ftc.gov.

Martin Ford "Mobile Apps and the Future of Shopping," *Huffington Post*, December 14, 2012. www.huffingtonpost.com.

Al Franken "Sen. Franken's 'Stalking Apps' Bill One Step Closer to Becoming Law," Franken.Senate.gov, December 13, 2012. www.franken.senate.gov.

Linsey Fryatt "The New App Economy—10 Reasons Why the Future of Business Is Indisputably Mobile," *Venture Village*, November 7, 2012. http://venturevillage.eu.

Joshua Gans "Does the App Economy Need Institutions?" Digitopoly, November 19, 2012. www.digitopoly.org.

Sam Grobart "Six Steps to Decluttering Your Smartphone," *New York Times*, June 13, 2012. www.nytimes.com.

Grant Gross "California AG: Mobile Apps Should Limit Data Collection," *ComputerWorld*, January 10, 2013. http://news.idg.no.

Juliana Gruenwald "Techies to Congress: Hands Off the Apps!" *National Journal*, September 12, 2012. www.nationaljournal.com.

Matthew Guay   "The Diverse and Changing World of
                     Apps," *AppStorm*, July 17, 2011.
                     http://web.appstorm.net.

M. Headd   "The App Economy and Government
                     as a Platform," *Civic Innovations*,
                     November 18, 2012. http://civic.io.

Huffington Post   "Google Apps Inaccessible to Blind
                     Students," March 15, 2011.
                     www.huffingtonpost.com.

Mike James   "The Disastrous Fragmentation of
                     Web Apps," *I Programmer*, October
                     26, 2012. www.i-programmer.info.

Tom Kaneshige   "Apple App Store's Dirty Little
                     Secret," *CIO*, February 22, 2010.
                     www.cio.com.

Ryan Kim   "App Stores Are Suffering from the
                     Tyranny of the Charts," *Gigaom*,
                     September 21, 2012. http://gigaom
                     .com.

Thilo Koslowski   "Forget the Internet of Things: Here
                     Comes the 'Internet of Cars'," *Wired*,
                     January 4, 2012. www.wired.com.

Michael Mandel   "What the App Economy Can Teach
                     the Whole Economy," *The Atlantic*,
                     February 22, 2012.
                     www.theatlantic.com.

Michael Mandel   "The Geography of the App
and Judith   Economy," CTIA: The Wireless
Scherer   Association, September 20, 2012.

Farhad Manjoo	"Fear Your Smartphone," *Slate*, December 2, 2011. www.slate.com.
Carla Naumburg	"Why I Deleted the Apps on My iPhone," *PsychCentral*, October 24, 2012. http://blogs.psychcentral.com.
Carla Naumburg	"I Put the Apps Back on My iPhone," *PsychCentral*, March 18, 2013. http//blogs.psychcentral.com.
OnGuardOnline .gov	"Understanding Mobile Apps," September 2011. http://onguard online.gov.
Avril Salter	"What Makes a Great Mobile Cloud App?" *Petri IT Knowledgebase*, May 7, 2012. www.petri.co.il.
Gerry Shih and Alexei Oreskovic	"Youth Flock to Mobile Messaging Apps May Be Threat to Facebook," Reuters, March 31, 2013. www.reuters .com.
David Streitfeld	"As Boom Lures App Creators, Tough Part Is Making A Living," *New York Times*, November 17, 2012. www.nytimes.com.
Derek Thompson	"The Amazing High-Speed Rise of the App Economy," *Atlantic*, February 8, 2012. www.theatlantic.com.
Cesar Torres	"Path Addresses Privacy Controversy, but Social Apps Remain a Risk to Users," *Ars Technica*, February 12, 2012. http://arstechnica.com.

Anton Troianovski
"Feathers Fly as New Rules Loom for Kids' Apps," *Wall Street Journal*, April 4, 2013. http://online.wsj.com.

Hayley Tsukayama
"Obama Campaign App Concerns Some Privacy Advocates," *Washington Post*, August 7, 2011. www.washingtonpost.com.

US Senate Judiciary Committee Subcommittee on Privacy, Technology, and the Law
"Protecting Mobile Privacy: Your Smartphones, Tablets, Cell Phones and Your Privacy," May 10, 2011. www.judiciary.senate.gov.

VisionMobile
"The New Mobile App Economy," June 2012. www.visionmobile.com.

Rolfe Winkler
"Apps Fall Far from Apple's Tree," *Wall Street Journal*, April 3, 2013. http://online.wsj.com.

Jenna Wortham
"Are We Suffering from Mobile App Burnout?" *New York Times* blog, February 15, 2013. http://bits.blogs.nytimes.com.

Index

D

E

F